W9-BXR-059

The Shadow in America

Reclaiming the Soul of a Nation

Compiled and Edited by
JEREMIAH ABRAMS

NATARAJ
PUBLISHING

THE SHADOW IN AMERICA
Reclaiming the Soul of a Nation

© 1994 Jeremiah Abrams

Published by Nataraj Publishing
1561 S. Novato Blvd.
Novato, CA 94947

Cover art and design by Lightbourne Images
Typography by **T:H**Typecast, Inc.

All rights reserved. This book may not be reproduced in whole or in part, without written permission from the publisher, except by a reviewer who may quote brief passages in a review; nor may any part of this book be reproduced, stored in a retrieval system, or transmitted in any form or by any means electronic, mechanical, photocopying, recording, or other, without written permission from the publisher.

The author of this book does not dispense medical advice nor prescribe the use of any technique as a form of treatment for physical or mental problems without the advice of a physician either directly or indirectly. In the event you use any of the information in this book, neither the author nor the publisher can assume any responsibility for your actions. The intent of the author is only to offer information of a general nature to help you in your quest for personal growth.

Library of Congress Cataloging-in-Publication Data

The shadow in America : reclaiming the soul of a nation / compiled and
  edited by Jeremiah Abrams.
      p.   cm.
    Includes bibliographical references.
    ISBN 1-882591-17-8 (alk. paper) : $12.95
      1. Shadow (Psychoanalysis)—Social aspects—United States.
    2. United States—social life and customs—Psychological aspects.
    3. United States—History—Psychological aspects.   4. Psychoanalysis
    and culture—United States.   I. Abrams, Jeremiah.
    BF175.5S55S48   1994
    155.8'973—dc20   94-27896
                                                                  CIP

First printing, November 1994
Printed in the U.S.A.
on acid-free recycled paper.

10   9   8   7   6   5   4   3   2   1

Awake! awake o sleeper of the land of shadows, wake!
expand!
I am in you and you are in me, mutual in love . . .
Fibers of love from man to man . . .
Lo! we are One.

—William Blake

Contents

To my father

Irving George Abrams

A warm heart and the charisma of faith:
These regards last longer than life.

Acknowledgments

I would like to thank the following people for their extraordinary support during the creation of this book: Joel Covitz, for his tireless understanding; Bob Stein, for his belief in this project from its inception, and for always being "on"; Linda Piscitelli Wolf, who believes in me; the Nataraj Team—especially Jim, Shakti, and Jane —for giving life to the project, and for doing business with integrity; Tom Valente, for the opportunity to try these ideas in a conference format; Hal Zina Bennett, for being the craftiest of editors; and my personal support team, without whom this book would not be—my children, Rachael and Phillip.

Of course, an endeavor such as this would not be possible without the generous participation of the contributors. I have enjoyed and continue to value my contact with each one, and I honor them here.

Jeremiah Abrams
Inverness, California
August 1994

The Mt. Vision Institute
Box 181
Inverness, CA 94937-0181

Foreword

THOMAS MOORE

AS PATRICIA BERRY IMPLIES IN HER ESSAY in this volume, if you're going to talk about shadow, you should be mindful of the very shadow of what you're saying. After all, why do we write and talk about shadow, except to find a way to outwit or evade it through understanding, awareness, consciousness, and psychological sophistication. At the outset of any discussion of shadow, it might be good to take note of our purposes and motivations. Even the slightest wish to be free of the taint of shadow is enough to soil our work and give it more of the very shadow we're trying to avoid.

Many writers who address shadow advocate "integrating" the shadow. The idea is to become conscious of material that is darkly objectionable or "close to consciousness" and bring it somehow within the realm of conscious living, thereby redeeming it and harnessing its potential for good. I'm suspicious of this approach because it appears too much like a clever way of painting the dark light, so that in the end it's really the light that serves us, not the dark.

An alternative approach would be to find ways to respect the dark as such, and to live with our murky understanding of its value. The trouble with consciousness, understanding, and

1

good will is that they can become an unbearable lightness, a partial life, and a sentimental stance. We need the dark to fill out the wide range of possibility, and to keep our good intentions honest. Besides, the intention to be good can often serve as an excuse for doing evil: having an image of ourselves without shadow, we are free to immerse ourselves in evil. The impressive (and depressing) list of outrageous evil deeds in America's past that Jeremiah Abrams presents in his title essay stands in strong contrast to the image Americans have of their own good will and intentions.

For many of us, one of the most effective ways of dealing with shadow is to allow our best intentions to be corroded: to realize that the world is not divided into the good and the bad with ourselves on the side of good. Dealing with shadow may mean not integrating or understanding it, not even appreciating it, but letting life's dark powers affect us, deepen the color of our self-image, and smudge the habitual bright way we judge our own wishes and actions. Ultimately, dealing with shadow is not an intellectual operation at all, but an emotional and ontological one. I don't think we realize the extent to which our habit of intellectualizing everything, and especially shadow, is a means of protecting ourselves from the challenges offered.

Our way of imagining shadow should not be too personal, thinking that shadow exists as compensation for the bright choices we have made in our own lives. Nor should we imagine the archetypal shadow too generally and abstractly. Every single thing has its shadow, and in order to allow shadow to be fully in life—which is how I imagine dealing with it—we have to allow and invite the emotions, the meanings, and the activities of each thing's shadow. Only by letting it exist fully in our world and in our lives does the good in its makeup become available to us.

The literal evil we see around us and in our past is not an example of too much shadow, but of too little. Real shadow is a constructive part of life, and it is a major portion of soul. The literal evils we see exist in a world trying to avoid shadow. I fear that the more we Americans insist on grand, wholesome notions of who we are and what our motives are, the further removed from gifts of shadow we will become, and in that way we will become even more sentimental and irresponsible—primary characteristics of shadowlessness.

We may have to reconsider our tendency to imprison, make illegal, ostracize, and emotionally deny the many difficult expressions of shadow we see in our culture. We could revision our own history in view of shadow by admitting to greed, violence, chauvinism, prejudice, and many other shadow qualities, which are literally harmful only when they are gilded with sophisticated evasions or excuses. As a nation among nations, we could give up superficial justifications and rationalizations for our shadow actions. Such justifications are a sign of the avoidance of soul, and the result can only be a soulless, symptom-ridden society.

Shadow is a great mystery, perhaps the greatest of all. Let us not try to deal with it by explaining it or offering theories about it. What is needed, as in the case of any mystery, is a pious, respectful attitude, as well as rituals for acknowledging its power, its place in life, and its absolute depth. We could use language that keeps its mystery intact, that shows how we are under its spell, and that admits we will never get it under our control—intellectually, emotionally, or practically.

Feeling the impact of some dark, aggressive action the American government takes, for example, we could proclaim a day of mourning, go to our churches and meditation rooms, cut some medallions, and paint some expiatory murals, rather than offer sophisticated reasons that attempt, perhaps uncon-sciously, to lighten the darkness or lessen our guilt. Real guilt, not a chronic feeling of guiltiness, is an effective weight for keeping us in this life with soul. It is a way of bearing shadow, a much more effective way than carving out a classification for shadow too precise and theoretical to bring into life.

Shadow, pure and simple, unpsychologized and unre-deemed, is one of the greatest gifts of soul. Whatever it takes to lead us toward respect for that mystery is one of the most effec-tive paths to soul available to us. Taking that path may entail some radical reversals in our thinking and acting, but all indi-cations in society, from war to crime, point to a need for just such a reversal. Our usual hygienic approach gets us nowhere with these social problems.

Nothing could be more important, then, than a book on our nation's shadow. Such a book is a gift more important than all our sentimental volumes of self-improvement combined. Gathering together in one volume visionaries who do not take an ideological approach to shadow and allowing them to speak in their own style about their own society is a project that speaks not only about soul, but also with soul.

Closely studying America's shadow does not automatically require self-pity, moralism, or negativity of any kind. America's shadow is a huge pile of fertilizer begging to be spread over all our institutions to help them get rooted and then to blossom. Americans are accustomed to dealing with our problems by reaffirming our decency, gathering together our can-do experts, and putting our efforts into grand projects of self-improvement. This book gives us hints toward another approach that could be much more effective—affirming our indecency, realizing that our shadow is impervious to expert analysis, and giving up altogether the project of ultimate self-improvement.

Reflecting on the shadow of our talk about shadow, we may find that at some level and in some small way at least, we are aiming at a life without shadow. I suspect that shadow is not close to consciousness at all; that very fantasy may be an apotropaic formula allowing us to believe that we can readily deal with shadow by ushering it directly into life. Perhaps shadow is always more profound than that, not nearly so close to human life, but rather divine, devilish, and truly archetypal. Religion may offer the only way to live in its precincts; certainly rationalism is inadequate. Religion could teach us to respect such a mystery and discover means of propitiating it—with the spirit of sacrifice and ritual. Propitiation means to acknowledge its superior power and its mystery, while hoping to be spared its literal destructiveness. In this way we might learn the paradox by which human life is graced by shadow only to the extent that we embrace it fully intact.

Preface

JEREMIAH ABRAMS

At this very moment in the history of humankind,
evolution has put us on the spot. There is an urgent
biological imperative to make the shadow conscious.
The moral burden of this immense task is greater than
any previous generation could have even conceived:
the destiny of the planet and our entire solar system.
Only by coming to terms with our nature—and the
nature of the Shadow—can we hope to avert total
catastrophe.

—Anthony Stevens

In the society of men the truth resides now less in what
things are than in what they are not. Our social
realities are so ugly if seen in the light of exiled truth,
and beauty is almost no longer possible if it is not a lie.

—R. D. Laing

TODAY, WE AMERICANS are faced with the cumulative
effects of many generations of denial and neglect, the
bloodline of an idealism that is masking dark propensities of
our own human nature. The American ethos, an endearing yet
naive tendency to deny one's own share of human imperfection, has finally become a collective burden, embedded in our
institutions, in our nation's policies, and even in what we'd like
to believe is our "individualistic" national character. In a very

real way, the postmodern psychology of American culture in the 1990s is a "shadow psychology," and the story of our national "soul" is a shadow story.

The Unredeemed American Shadow

UNWITTINGLY, THOSE AMERICANS WHO PRECEDED US have bought themselves time by borrowing against our generation and those to follow us. Consequently, we are both the beneficiaries of their good intentions *and* the bearers of their unredeemed shadowy choices. This is a simple truth, with no intention to fix blame. Today, the excesses we have inherited are reflected in our federal government's fiscal policies; the deficit has become our national symbol, the residual of our "blind-side economics," ruled by a strategy of "spend now, pay later." On many fronts, *later has arrived.* The price for the American dream has escalated and cannot be measured in mere dollars.

In many respects, we have borrowed in suffering and mortgaged our futures and those of our children. The list of transgressions is a modern jeremiad: our cities are overcrowded and deteriorating, our schools are bankrupt, our poor are homeless, our people demoralized, our government inefficient, our politicians corrupt, our economy the prey of foreign investors, our major industries leveraged out by modern-day "privateers," our ground waters polluted, our forests choked and dying, our oceans depleted of life, our natural resources squandered, our environment degraded, our biosphere damaged, our air fouled, our agriculture toxified, our wildlife threatened, our daily lives harried and rushed.

What we need is a psychological approach that can alert every citizen to the dire consequences of our unchecked and unacknowledged darker side. A deep psychological force is at work in our world, and a deep psychological solution is necessary. As the ancient Greek dictum reminds us, "The god that wounds, heals."

Recently, my six-year-old son Phillip and I saw the environmental advocate Jacques Cousteau detail accounts of how we are exhausting the oceanic environment of our planet. The pictures of a denuded Haiti and the death of the coral reefs frightened Phillip. We had just returned from a trip to western Canada where forestry clear-cutting has become a controversial issue. He had witnessed such devastation firsthand. My boy asked me, "Dad, is this for real? Why are they doing this? Is it for money? Are the people who are doing this greedy?"

I didn't know exactly how to answer him. Frankly, I was dumb-founded by his perceptive and precocious questions. In Phillip's young mind, a pattern is beginning to emerge.

I searched for the words to explain to him that the human ego is currently the most destructive force on the face of the earth. But, as contradictory as it may seem, the human alter ego, the unconscious complement of the ego—the shadow— holds our saving grace.

Pulling the Evolutionary Trigger

AS A SOCIETY, WE ARE FORCED TO FACE our infatuation with the light. This is actually an unprecedented opportunity for America to mature as a nation, to make the difficult but just choices, to undertake the right actions. Most recently, the implosion of shadow energies in our culture has been ignited by the loss of our traditional Cold War enemies. It is no longer so easy to create foreign intrigues to distract us from our own troubles. America is waking up to the reality that our problems are not just the result of an economic slump but the result of a long history of *denial*, of accumulated darkness, that has been so thoroughly integrated into our national character that it's become virtually invisible to us.

Today, virtually all our heroes have clay feet; we are seeing them more clearly. The hero of our last war was not able to pull off the sleight of hand that would have won him his presidential reelection bid. Americans are not in a total stupor. Why, we can't even find a good enemy anymore, someone to blame for all these miseries. We have no one to blame, no one to punish, no way to expiate our guilt. Shadow psychology implies that we can't turn away or project our own human weaknesses onto others. We don't have the option to rationalize or make excuses—we have come too far, our parents have taught us too well. If we are not totally jaded and cynical, we can meet our *own* generation's failures, and proclaim all the while, "*Mea Culpa! Mea Culpa!*" Like Walt Kelly's Pogo, we can appropriately say, "We have met the enemy and he is us."

There is an undeniable imperative for America: it is time for us to come clean. The shadowy denied parts of our fragile idealism are staring back at us, bringing the blush of shame and guilt as we look into the faces of the homeless, into the disappointed eyes of our children, and into our own sober reflections. If only we can find the courage, and take on the challenge of our own share of the darkness, we might just pull the evolutionary trigger in our collective awareness, and begin to reaffirm, with grace, the human experiment.

A Roundtable Discussion

PSYCHOLOGY IS MOVING OUT OF THE CONSULTING ROOM and into the world. These essays—all revolving around the specific theme of the Shadow—focus on the practical uses and applications of greater psychological awareness. The collection reads best as a roundtable discussion, a group of nine thoughtful individuals bringing the full force of intellect and feeling to their subject, engaging in *personal* dialogue about the state of our culture and where we seem to be going.

Each author, a participant in American life, has focused on that piece of their experience that is relevant here. Each is interested in elevating and respecting the shadow qualities in our lives, in recognizing that shadow has an important place. Rather than purging the darkness, each of these essays identifies a piece of shadow power in modern American life.

Three of these essays were originally presented during a conference at the Omega Institute at Rhinebeck, New York. I had the idea that it might be interesting to invite presenters to participate in a dialogue about the collective shadow in America. I asked each to present a paper on an agreed-upon topic and later prepare the material for publication. These three are joined by seven other writers I felt could make a valuable contribution to our understanding of the subject. Taken together, these essays round out a picture of shadow in culture, a descriptive more than an ideological framework, ranging from environmental concerns, to interpersonal and intrapersonal life, to sex and religion, to pleasure and addiction, to money and work, to racism and prejudice, to politics and diplomacy.

Each of these essays reflects the sensibility of its author, and there has been no attempt to homogenize the writing or the ideas for consistency from one writer to the next. I have provided introductions to each part, a narrative thread running through the text to orient the reader and to provide deep background. Some pieces may have more appeal than others, some may be more difficult or produce less resonance. Rather than read the book consumptively, cover to cover, the reader is encouraged to "graze," to find what piques your interest, what provokes your own psychology and your own shadow awareness. With some essays, you will need to proceed slowly and remember that, in places, the material presented is more dense with substance, perhaps more provocative of shadow.

Part I, *Shadow and Culture*, sounds the keynote, echoing the address I gave at the Omega conference. Here I present a brief history of the shadow concept, personal versus collective shadows, and provide a context for thinking about shadow, particularly the American shadow.

Part II, *Shadow Awareness*, consists of an essay, "Light and Shadow," in the strong yet personal voice of its author, Patricia Berry. Pat first delivered this piece at the Rhinebeck conference; it contains several perspectives on the nature of the American shadow: that of a young woman living abroad, that of a Jungian analyst concerned with the challenges of her profession, and that of a woman with deep psychological clarity who is cautious about the ways in which we can fool ourselves, even with shadow awareness. "What we really need," she says, "is an awareness of the shadow of shadow awareness."

Part III, *Between Masculine and Feminine*, features a narrative, "Gender Wars," written by the couple Aaron Kipnis and Elizabeth Herron. It is the partial story of a retreat experience in the mountain wilderness of California. Here they capture the immediacy of one of their workshops in gender reconciliation. This particular week-long encounter was facilitated by the authors for seven men and seven women at lakeside, high in the Sierra Nevada. They recount for us the shadow portions of dialogues amongst the women, amongst the men, and in mixed company. This essay has been excerpted from Aaron and Liz's recent book, *Gender War, Gender Peace: The Quest for Justice Between Women and Men*.

Part IV, *Sexuality*, comprises the essay, "Sexuality, Shadow, and the Holy Bible," senior Jungian analyst Robert M. Stein presented at the Omega Institute conference. Here we explore with him the mind/body/soul split, a theme that he has been studying and writing about, with increasing force and clarity, for the past twenty years. He writes of the great power of sexuality and how Puritan and Christian fundamentalist projections of the archetypal shadow (Evil) onto sexuality have corrupted our instinctual connection with our bodies. "With the demise of communism and the withdrawal of the projection of Evil onto Russia," he writes, " sexuality has once again been reinstated as the Devil . . . Even the tragedy of AIDS is being used to reinforce our puritanical attitudes toward sexuality."

Part V, *Addiction*, features the essay "Sacred Hunger: Shadow, Ecstasy, and Addiction," which is distilled from the work of writer and teacher Jacquelyn Small. Jacquie has worked to move addiction and recovery treatment services out from the influence of the symptom-ridden medical model, toward transpersonal psychology and what she calls "psycho-spiritual integration." "Addiction can be viewed as the shadow running out of control, as untamed libido . . ." she writes. "We don't just *manage* our libido, we can transform it. We must work on assimilating the positive quality that is trying to emerge from untamed libido. This is how we view healing from addiction in our work." This essay comes from her latest book, *Embodying Spirit: Coming Alive with Meaning and Purpose*.

Part VI, *Money*, contains the essay "The Moneyed Society," which comes from archetypal psychologist Robert Sardello. It is a stirring and funny piece, filled with scatology and anecdote about money, work, and worth, about the strong and complex grasp money has on us. We need help to imagine about money. "Without an imagination of money the world remains lifeless," says Dr. Sardello. This essay was published in another form in the 1983 book, *Money and the Soul of the World*.

Part VII, *Prejudice*, consists of two essays. The first, "The Scapegoat Archetype," is by Jungian analyst Sylvia Brinton Perera, from her book, *The Scapegoat Complex: Toward a Mythology of Shadow and Guilt*. This is a definitive work, giving us a foundation for understanding the pervasive shadow complex and its common expression in prejudice, racism, and genocide. "Scapegoating, as it is currently practiced," Perera writes, "means finding the one or ones who can be identified with evil or wrong-doing, blamed for it, and cast out from the community in order to leave the remaining members with a feeling of guiltlessness, atoned (at-one) with the collective standards of behavior."

The second essay in Part VII, "An Archetypal Dilemma: The LA Riots," is a piece of applied psychology by Jungian analyst Jerome S. Bernstein. It moves out of the world of theory and the consulting room, taking us into the heart of the beast, revealing the disease of racism in contemporary American life and illustrating the catastrophic consequences of our unchecked cultural shadow.

Part VIII, *Shadow Poetics*, features two new poems by Robert Bly. Robert's long-standing interest in the shadow was captured in 1988 in *A Little Book on the Human Shadow*, a book adapted from several live readings, presentations and interviews. In recent years, Bly has garnered attention through his mythopoetic book, *Iron John*, which has become a manifesto for awakened consciousness among American men. Robert is still first and foremost a poet, and his shadow sensibility—wedded to the power of his poetry—provides us with a thought provoking epilogue.

Shadow Reminders: Remember to Remember When You Remember

TO ACCEPT SHADOW MEANS accepting the inherent ambiguities in life. We need to honor shadow, make it a part of us, not banish it, or heal it, or be dominated by it. An important result of shadow work, perhaps the most important, is the growing development of *compassion*, the opening of one's heart, the real and actual acceptance and love of others specifically for that piece of humanity's imperfection which they carry. In what we don't accept about ourselves and others—what we individually or collectively deny, exile, or project—there lies the possiblility to discover our fuller humanity.

Shadow work is heart work. It operates on the principle "As above, so below": if something happens inside then it also becomes real outside. If enough of us carry our share of the darkness and open ourselves compassionately to the world around us, then—as a nation and as individuals—we add to the critical mass of awareness that is helping to create a compassionate culture, one that can tolerate paradox and ambiguity, one that allows these qualities to coexist with order and clarity. "What gives soul to people," said the Greek psychologist Evangelos Christou, "is the capacity to experience the paradox of life."

Shadow work *is* soul work. And the frontier where we confront the shadow is, as it has always been, within one's own sphere of influence, within one's personal sense of joy and suffering, within the individual soul. We need to invoke the Greek god Hermes, who governs shadow work; we need to honor the archetype that serves the dual roles of messenger (bearing the truths of the gods and goddesses) and trickster, who guides souls to Hades, helping us to cross over and clearly see the other side of things, the underbelly of life.

It isn't enough to merely have insight into the shadow. To "understand" can be the kiss of death. One cannot just know the ideas, and turn this psychological approach into an intellectual game. Ultimately, what is essential is that we walk all the talk, *apply* the insight, *embody* our awareness in action. Otherwise, shadow awareness just creates *more* shadow. The writer Henry Miller, a true American cut from the cloth of individualism, reminds us that "The full and joyful acceptance of the worst in oneself may be the only sure way of transforming it." As Miller also once said of the role of the artist, the purpose of shadow work is "to inoculate the world with disillusionment."

Shadow work demands that we persist at unifying our awareness. Like the practice called the "Middle Way" in Buddhism, shadow integration is an enabling, unifying awareness which allows us to reduce the shadow's inhibiting or destructive potentials, releasing trapped positive life energies that might otherwise be caught in the pretense and posturing required to conceal the shadow. It is, above all, a humbling experience. The Buddhists say that we should never get rid of our negative energy; rather we should *transform* it into the energy of enlightenment. We need to remember this principle in our everyday lives, especially when we are wrestling with circumstances that are too ambiguous to tolerate. The contemporary Tibetan Buddhist teacher Sogyal Rinpoche says that we must "Remember to remember when we remember."

To go in the dark with a light is to
     know the light.
To know the dark, go dark.
Go without sight, and find that the dark, too,
     blooms and sings,
and is traveled by dark feet and dark wings.

—Wendell Berry

PART I

Shadow
and Culture

The Shadow in America

JEREMIAH ABRAMS

> We live in a time when there dawns upon us a
> realization that the people living on the other side
> of the mountain are not made up exclusively of
> red-headed devils responsible for all the evil on this
> side of the mountain.
>
> —C. G. Jung

> Being human, especially being a self-aware human,
> entails facing bitter truths about existence. The price
> one pays for self-awareness is to see the dark side—not
> so much to dwell there, but to penetrate, to somehow
> get through and actually affirm your destiny.
>
> —Irvin Yalom

WE OWE A DEBT TO C. G. JUNG for giving us the imaginative concept "realizing the shadow." His desire to remain free of rigidity in his thinking led him to choose language with a more poetic precision. Jung valued the imaginal, saying that "Image is Psyche"—it is in our imaginings we will find our souls. [1]

As early as 1912, while still under the influence of Freud's theories, Jung uses the phrase "shadow side of the psyche" to characterize our "not recognized desires" and the "repressed portions of the personality."[2] He is suggesting at this point something akin to the dark side of the moon, a quality of the person that is unseen but nevertheless real. In his 1917 essay, "On the Psychology of the Unconscious," Jung speaks of the personal shadow as the *other* in us, a splinter personality, a reprehensible inferior part by which we may be embarrassed or shamed, a hidden disposition appearing in our dreams, frequently as a contra-personage of the same sex: "By shadow I mean the 'negative' side of the personality, the sum of all those unpleasant qualities we like to hide, together with the insufficiently developed functions and the content of the personal unconscious."[3]

By 1945, Jung is referring to the shadow as simply "the thing a person has no wish to be."[4] "One does not become enlightened," he said, "by imagining figures of light, but by making the darkness conscious. The latter procedure, however, is disagreeable and therefore not popular."[5]

In his 1946 essay "On the Nature of the Psyche," Jung speaks reflectively about realization of the shadow, calling it "an eminently practical problem . . . which should not be twisted into an intellectual activity, for it has far more the meaning of a suffering and a passion that implicate the whole man." He goes on to say:

> The essence of that which has to be realized and assimilated has been expressed so trenchantly and so plastically in poetic language by the word "shadow" that it would be almost presumptuous not to avail oneself of this linguistic heritage.
>
> Even the term "inferior part of the personality" is inadequate and misleading, whereas "shadow" presumes nothing that would rigidly fix its content. The "man without a shadow" is statistically the commonest human type, one who imagines he actually is only what he cares to know about himself. Unfortunately neither the so-called religious man nor the man of scientific pretensions forms any exception to this rule.[6]

With regard to the formulation of the concept of the Shadow, Jung's linguistic sensibility was clearly informed by his reverence for the work of Johann Wolfgang von Goethe, whose Dr. Faustus was a model of the scientific man coming to terms with the darker forces in life. There is no doubt that Jung was also influenced by 19th century German Romantic literature, where the most popular motif was that of the *doppelganger*, or mirror image, the idea being that there is another one of us running around somewhere, whether we know it or not, a double with opposite characteristics. Jung was also intensely interested in comparative mythology, where he found the theme of evil to be universal in classical and folk myths in every culture. His research provided an empirical basis for his ideas about shadow and evil in the individual and in the collective psyche.

Jung's use of the term "shadow" was undoubtedly also influenced by Gustav Fechner, a German experimental psychologist whose work Jung frequently cited. Fechner wrote playfully about the reality of the actual physical shadow we cast—the play of light and shadow—personifying it and giving the shadow both speech and volition. In his essay "The Shadow is Alive," published in the 1880s, Fechner wrote, "The sensitive person who goes before the populace can see what the rest cannot notice. In the same way, the shadow may see much that may escape our eyes."[7]

Everything with Substance Casts a Shadow

FOR JUNG, REALIZATION OF THE SHADOW was the *Gesellenstuck*, the journeyman's apprentice-work, a prerequisite for pursuit of the psychological life. He concluded that dealing with shadow and evil is ultimately an "individual secret" (his words*)*—equal to that of experiencing God—and so powerful an experience that it can transform the whole person. "We each must rediscover a deeper source of our own spiritual life," he reasoned. "To do this we are obliged to struggle with evil, to confront the shadow, to integrate the devil. There is no other choice."

The shadow is negative, but negative only from the vantage point of consciousness. It is not—as Freud insisted—totally immoral and incompatible with our conscious personalities. Rather, it potentially contains values of the highest morality. This is particularly true when there is a side hidden in the shadow personality which society values as positive, yet which is regarded by the individual as inferior. The shadow most closely approaches what Freud understood as "the repressed." But in contrast to the Freudian view, Jung's shadow is an inferior personality that has its own contents, such as autonomous thought, ideas, images, and value judgments, that are similar to the superior conscious personality.[8]

Today, the term "shadow" indicates that part of the unconscious psyche that is thought to be nearest to consciousness, even though it is not completely accepted by it. Because it is contrary to our chosen conscious attitude, the shadow personality is denied expression in life and coalesces into a relatively separate personality in the unconscious, where it is isolated from exposure and discovery. For Jung and those who follow his mode, psychotherapy offers a ritual for transformation and renewal in which the shadow personality can be brought to awareness and assimilated. Shadow work is not about dismantling the personal shadow, but rather refers to the ongoing process of balancing and depolarizing, healing the split between our conscious sense of self and all else we might be, like the practice called "The Middle Way" in Buddhism. Shadow integration means developing

the capacity to carry an expanded and more unified awareness, enabling us to reduce the shadow's inhibiting or
destructive potentials and to release trapped, positive life
energies that may be caught in the pretense and posturing
required to conceal the shadow.

What is the shadow? While Jung finally defined the shadow
as "the thing one has no wish to be," we continue to know it by
many names: the alter ego, the lower self, the other, the double,
the dark twin, the disowned self, the repressed self, the id, etc.
We speak of "meeting our demons," "wrestling with the
devil," ("the devil made me do it"), a "descent to the underworld," a "dark night of the soul," a "midlife crisis." The
shadow abounds in the classic human stories: it is a Grendl to
his Beowulf, Shakespeare's Macbeth to his more noble
Hamlet, Mephistopheles in dialogue with Faust, Darth Vader
(the "dark father") in battle with his ego-heroic son, Luke
Skywalker.

Shadow refers to that portion of us that is constantly shifting and changing in the light of our ego-consciousness, those
aspects of self and culture that we fail to bring fully to responsible awareness. As individuals and as members of a specific
culture, we are continually and viscerally selecting and editing
experience, creating an ego-based ideal of self and world. But
everything with substance casts a shadow; each of us, through
the light of our own ego awareness, generates shadow. Ego and
alter ego, national pride and international disgrace, humanitar-
ian good and human evil, power and love: "One is but the
shadow of the other," said Jung.

Where does shadow originate? How is it created? It begins
to take form very early in our lives—beginning with the "first
emancipation of an "I" from the great sea of unconsciousness."[9] It is that portion of our thoughts, feelings, and

experiences that we repress in favor of an idealized self, an ego ideal. This rejected part doesn't go away, however. Instead, it is carefully hidden away in the unconscious part of our personalities, a shadow subpersonality. What doesn't fit the reinforced ideal of the developing ego becomes shadow. According to John Sanford, the Jungian analyst and Episcopal minister, "The shadow is always an aspect of the ego itself, the qualities of the shadow could have become part of the structure of the ego. You might say the shadow is like the ego's brother or sister, and not necessarily a sinister figure."[10]

Poet Robert Bly, in his *A Little Book on the Human Shadow*, calls the shadow the "long bag we drag behind us." (It's curious and encouraging that today our poets are giving us psychological prose about the shadow!). Bly says, "We spend our life until we're twenty deciding what parts of ourselves to put in the bag, and we spend the rest of our lives trying to get them out again."[11]

Robert Johnson, a writer and lecturer who has brought Jungian concepts to lay audiences, recently has written, "We divide the self into an ego and a shadow because our culture insists that we behave in a particular manner. This is our legacy from having eaten of the fruit of the tree of knowledge in the Garden of Eden. Culture takes away the simple human in us, but gives us more complex and sophisticated power."

"The civilizing process," Johnson says, "which is the brightest achievement of humankind, consists of culling out those characteristics that are dangerous to the smooth functioning of our ideals. Anyone who does not go through this process remains a 'primitive' and can have no place in a cultivated society."[12]

The Collective Shadow

GROUPS AND CULTURES HAVE IDEALS AS WELL, and these in turn produce shadow, the dark side of the collective ideal. Both personal and collective shadows have a valuable function in that ego and collective ideals are fallacious and one-sided. Just as the personal shadow works within the individual personality by compensating destructively against ego-ideals, so too does the collective shadow seek to demolish collective ideals. Were our inflated ideals not continually being eaten from the depths of the human soul, as Johnson and others suggest, there would be no development, individually or collectively.

So we begin to see how national identities can have shadows as well. Can you see the destructive force of Nazism as an expression of the German shadow (as Jung suggested in vain), the returning vengeance of a repressed and enraged god (Wotan) in the German psyche? Was shadow not made visible to us in the Khmer Rouge's genocidal plunder of Cambodia, as the barbarian Pol Pot erupted infectiously from the wounds of that nation (wounds which, incidentally, were inflicted by American armed forces)? Movements and governments are subject to the contagion of mental epidemics of immense proportions, rapidly spreading shadowy scourges, all in the name of a good cause.

The collective shadow—human evil in some malignant form—echoes back at us from virtually every direction: it shouts from newsstand headlines; it squats in the X-rated neon pornography shops on the periphery of our cities; it wanders our streets, sleeping in doorways, homeless; it embezzles our life savings from the local savings and loan; it corrupts power-hungry politicians; it perverts our systems of justice; it drives our military arsenals toward the brink of insanity; it sells arms to mad leaders and gives the profits to reactionary insurgents; it pours pollution through hidden pipes into our rivers and oceans and poisons our food with invisible pesticides; it steals the cash in leveraged buyouts and insider trading; it threatens our health with defective technology and false promises, with medical claims and disastrous side-effects.

These observations are not some new fundamentalism, thumping on a biblical version of reality. Our era has made forced witnesses of us all. "The whole world is watching." There is really no avoiding the frightening specter of satanic shadows, being acted out by political leaders, white-collar businessmen, and terrorists alike. Our inner desire to be whole—which is now made manifest in the machinery of an age of communication—forces us to face the conflicting hypocrisy that is everywhere in modern life, traveling at the speed of light.

Here we begin to see the mythic proportions of the shadow concept, the archetypal Shadow, the reality of evil. Just as we each contain a potential murderer or suicide as an inherent mode of human behavior, so the denied shame and rage of an entire generation can be released—through *participation mystique*—and engulf us all. We recognize the archetypal shadow in the great stories of humanity: now as the devil, here as Shiva, there as Loki, Beelzebub, and in the alchemists' *sol niger* (black sun). Freud called it *Thanatos*, the death instinct. Both Freud and Jung recognized this archetypal force as something which is simply there and cannot be rationalized away.

It was Heideigger who said, "The only thing we learn from history is that we don't learn from history." This remark acknowledges the plain truth that human actions do not necessarily proceed from rational motives. Denial of the great forces that lurk in the individual and collective unconscious produces the repetition compulsion seen in most human atrocities. Jung was wont to turn melancholic on this point. "We need more understanding of human nature," he said, "because the only real danger that exists is man himself. He is the great danger, and we are pitifully unaware of it. We know nothing of man, far too little. His psyche should be studied, because we are the origin of all coming evil."[13]

We own a legacy of human misfortune—of suffering released onto the world unconsciously and unwittingly—dispensed by people in service of a "just" or a "righteous" cause. Such miseries often have been much worse than any evils the perpetrators sought to eradicate. One only has to think of the Crusades against the infidels, a fight which is still being conducted today in the name of "ethnic cleansing" in the strife-ridden mountains of Bosnia-Herzegovina; or of the Vietnam War in our era, the effects of which we can still see on the streets of America, where at least 30 percent of our homeless population are veterans of "that nasty little war."

The Shadow in America

THE "FACTS" OF AMERICAN HISTORY can be viewed from the point of view of shadow behavior. Americans are, by and large, an idealistic people whose destiny has been shaped by waves of influences, each wave having been shaped, in turn, by some form of oppression or idealized hope, the kind of forces that have brought most people to these shores. Our institutions are founded on the highest principles of individual human dignity, the democratic ideal, with the objective of creating a better life for as many as possible. We have always held ourselves to be leaders in the world's pursuit of the just and fair society.

Throughout its history, the United States has struggled with the ideal versus the reality, with the hypocrisy that is bred by extreme idealism. Just to touch on a few low points in our nation's *less* glorious past, we might consider:

- the effects of Puritanism on our work ethic and sexual mores
- the witch hunts and the murders of thousands of women
- the slave trade, slavery, and their corollaries: the destruction wreaked by the Civil War, Jim Crow, and modern-day racism
- our imperialistic "Manifest Destiny" ambitions, expansionism, Native American genocide
- economic imperialism and the exploitation of third-world satellites
- the dark side of the free-enterprise system, epitomized by the robber barons
- exploitation of child labor and the co-optation of American labor unions
- militarism and isolationism
- McCarthyism and Red-baiting
- the military-industrial complex and its theater, the Cold War
- the Ugly American
- the Vietnam War and its legacy
- rampant consumerism and the resulting environmental degradation

These examples from our nation's history eventually have come round to reveal our collective hypocrisy, though too often too late.

In postmodern American society, we can see the growth of shadow excesses everywhere:

- in an uncontrolled power-drive for knowledge and for the domination of nature—expressed in the amorality of the sciences and in the unregulated marriage of business and technology;
- in a self-righteous compulsion to help and cure others— expressed in the abuse of the role of medicine, the greed of corporate hospitals, medical personnel and pharmaceutical companies, and in the codependent roles in the helping professions;
- in a fast-paced workplace—expressed in the apathy of an alienated workforce, in the unplanned obsolescence produced by automation, and in the hubris of success;
- in our maximization of growth and progress—expressed in leveraged buyouts, profiteering, insider trading, the S & L debacle, as well as pollution, ozone damage and unrestrained waste;
- in a materialistic hedonism—expressed in conspicuous consumption, exploitative advertising, and the resultant spiritual impoverishment;
- in our desire to control our intimate lives—expressed in widespread narcissistic behavior, exploitation of others, and the abuse of minorities, women and children;
- and in our ever-present fear of death—seen in obsessions with youthfulness, health, fitness, diet, drugs, and with longevity at any price.

These shadowy aspects run the width and breadth of our society. The tried solutions to our collective excess may be even more dastardly than the problems. Consider, for example, the reactionary horrors that have arisen in our century, fascism and authoritarianism, vain attempts to contain social disorder and what was widely perceived as decadence and permissiveness. More recently, the fervor of religious and political fundamentalism has reawakened throughout the world, arguably in response to progressive ideas, and encouraging, in W. B. Yeats' phrase, "mere anarchy to be loosed upon the world."

The shadow issues of America in the 1990s seem quite clear. How much longer can we deny them? I would suggest three themes of particular shadow intensity that have larger ramifications for the decade (these, of course, apply to the rest of the world to a greater or lesser extent, but I am speaking from the privileged perspective of an American):

1. Environmental Degradation: in giving overwhelming power to patriarchal consciousness and the doctrine of material progress, we have rejected the feminine principle of being. This has resulted in a cruelty and an arrogance toward our Great Mother, the earth. We are not destroying the planet; she will survive. Ultimately, we are destroying our own species, or at least our quality of life for the time being, and wantonly taking down many other life forms with us.

2. Alienation: in the workplace, in relationships, the continuing atomization of our society and the loss of soul-connection with each other. Especially deteriorated is the compassionate connection with the forgotten and the dispossessed, the underclass in America. In our era the care of the less fortunate and the attention to those individuals enduring hardship and suffering has been dismissed as liberal, and even as un-American. Mother Teresa, who has cared for the sick and needy of Calcutta for more than thirty years, has said, "America has a worse poverty than India's, and it's called loneliness."

3. Overpopulation: the major source of the conflict and violence
   underlying the distribution of planetary resources continues
   to be scarcity based on increasing demand. The problem—
   providing for more of humankind with diminished (and perhaps damaged) natural and human resources—seems unre-
   deemable. America's resources were once thought of as
   inexhausable, but now the burden of overpopulation is finally
   made manifest in our own urban areas, where we can see the
   effects on our strained and congested facilities, like sclerotic
   arteries in the body polis. Deteriorating municipal water quality has become a national problem, and may only be the
   canary in the mineshaft. Thomas Malthus was right, Paul
   Ehrlich is right. Americans have a mandate—it is, after all,
   our democratic ideal—to reorient our use of resources, time,
   and space, to participate in the global coordination of food
   production and distribution, to plan human environments to
   preserve the quality of life and bio-diversity. These are enormous and complex problems whose solutions are so perplex-
   ing that many cannot even think of such things, it causes too
   much anxiety. Yet, these are the tasks of a generation born
   into millenial change. Europe has taken a lead here, since conditions in the old world have worsened sooner. These problems are further complicated and magnified when we observe
   the influential effects of our consumer-oriented values and
   habits on the burgeoning cultures of the world—India,
   China, and Mexico, for example—which for now provide a
   frontier for inexpensive labor, but which continue to grow at
   alarming rates in their internal demand for the basics of life.

Encompassing the Shadowy Aspects

IT IS POSSIBLE FOR AN ENTIRE NATION to become self-
reflective and aware of the effects of its destructive shadow, and

then to repudiate them. Consider this example, which I cited in *Meeting the Shadow*.[14] It is from an article in the *Philadelphia Inquirer*, June 11, 1988, reporting that the Soviet government, under the leadership of Mikhail Gorbachev, was temporarily canceling all history exams throughout the country:

> The Soviet Union, saying history textbooks had taught genera-tions of Soviet children lies that poisoned their "minds and souls," announced yesterday that it had cancelled final history exams for more than 53 million students.
>
> Reporting the cancellation, the government newspaper Izvestia said the extraordinary decision was intended to end the passing of lies from generation to generation, a process that has consolidated the Stalinist political and economic system that the current leadership wants to end.
>
> ". . . The guilt of those who deluded one generation after another, poisoning their minds and souls with lies, is immeasur-able," the paper said in a front-page commentary.
>
> "Today, we are reaping the bitter fruits of our own moral lax-ity. We are paying for succumbing to conformity and thus to giv-ing silent approval of everything that now brings the blush of shame to our faces and about which we do not know how to answer our children honestly."[15]

Early in the perestroika era of the 1980s, Gorbachev was reported to have said to then-President Reagan, "I'm going to do something terrible to you; I'm going to take away your enemy." Indeed, Gorbachev kept his promise and took away our most favored shadow host. We find ourselves at a critical time in history. The Cold War has ended and the implosions of those shadow projections that were once carried by our traditional enemy are now upon us. We can easily search for new excesses or for new enemies to take up whatever we cannot bear to contain in our own collective awareness. It is no small irony that two months after the Berlin Wall came down, we were invading Panama. Within a year of these events we had committed 300,000 American troops to defend oil interests in the Mideast.

Domestically, we have only to look on our streets and see the failure of our ideals, witness the inertia that has set into our collective conscience, sabatoging the less fortunate among us. Racism and bigotry continue to seethe on the periphery, and appear on our news screens in updated guises—no longer white hooded robes and burning crosses, but replete with preppy garb, plastic surgery, and euphemisms. We are strained to the limits, as evidenced in such complex contemporary reactions as Japan-bashing, negative electioneering, anti-incumbency, or the Los Angeles riots. We need someone to blame for what isn't going right with us, and these sentiments can erupt suddenly, whether in the electoral process, in boardrooms, or on the streets of our cities.

Relatively speaking, America is a young country. Today, accelerating world events challenge us to examine the psychology of our idealism. In the absence of traditional enemies, without the threat from a nuclear arms race, and lacking the illusion of indomitable economic strength, we are forced to realize our culture's one-sidedness. It is in the spirit of our times to find a balance in the ways we Americans conduct ourselves, collectively and privately. Our culture's maturity—rather than its decline into some fearful millennial Armageddon—depends on it.

We must grapple with the forces that keep us from being fully human, that prevent our society and its individual citizens from acting on, and thus realizing, their ideals.

Everything has a shadow side. By learning to see, accept, and encompass the shadowy aspects of ourselves and our national identity, perhaps we can wake up and renew the promise of the American dream.

PART II

Shadow
Awareness

Introduction

The meeting with oneself is, at first, the meeting with
one's own shadow. The shadow is a tight passage, a
narrow door, whose painful constriction no one is
spared who goes down to the deep well.

—C. G. Jung

FROM EARLIEST TIMES, HUMANITY HAS STRUGGLED
with the problem of evil. The dark mysteries of life—the
unity of the cycles of birth and death, light and darkness, day
and night—have been externalized in our experience. No
longer are they mysteries, they have become polarities, turned
into "good" and "bad." Religions have helped us to struggle
with these oppositions, adding a moral effort and a spiritual
dimension to our understanding, all the while reinforcing the
dualistic perception of our world. Worldwide, the artists, sto-
rytellers, priests, priestesses, and healers have always reflected
these great themes back to us, challenging us to bring our
struggle with the unknown into awareness, to acknowledge and
confront the forces in life that give us the most trouble.

Perhaps the most troublesome human shadow is death
itself, our greatest mystery. In American life, death is the ultimate unknown, a source of anxiety which drives us beyond
religion to find security and peace of mind in visions of
immortality, in the worship of youthfulness, and in the new
religion of modern medical science. After all, America was

once thought by Europeans to be the great last hope for discovering the mythic fountain of youth. Our culture still carries that idealistic longing (as well as other hopes) for much of the Western world.

Today, we are confronted with the problem of evil in our shrinking global community. We see cruelty and greed blindly played out on a daily basis by governments, community leaders, corporations, and individuals alike. In this age of information, we cannot escape this knowledge. And along with our heightened awareness of these evils comes the inevitable fear and foreboding. Being better informed of the human capacity for evil has not seemed to ease our anxieties, though our curiousity has grown more morbid with the proliferation of news and information media. The age-old question, "Whence comes evil?" remains unanswered.

C. G. Jung's musings on the subject were not entirely pessimistic, according to Marie-Louise von Franz, who worked closely with Jung for over 25 years:

> Jung saw this present-day culmination of evil as typical of the historical catastrophes that tend to accompany the great transitions from one age to another, in our case the end of the Piscean age and the beginning of the Aquarian. In fact we are even menaced with a total eradication of life on our earth, either gradually, through the destruction of the environment, or through a global war. The increase in criminality, the occurrence of holocausts, and so on, are a first warning. Everyone is talking about these problems these days, and nobody knows what ought to be done. Apppeals to reason seem to echo away unheard . . . Jung also did not have a simple answer, but he was convinced that every individual who undertook to come to terms with the evil in himself would make a more effective contribution toward the salvation of the world than idealistic external machinations would. Here we are talking about more than just insight into one's personal shadow; we are speak-

ing also of a struggle with the dark side of God (or the Self), which the human being cannot face but must, as Job did.[1]

Facing evil in our country or in the world requires first facing it in ourselves. The task of realizing the shadow—what Jung called the "apprentice-work"—is an individual problem that has cultural consequences. All inner work—any psychological or spiritual development—begins with work upon the shadow. The shadow themes that run through our lives are too easily projected onto others and into solutions that involve the cooperation of the outer world; as long as we externalize our issues this way we are bound to feel powerless to effect or resolve the complexities of modern life. What, then, is our hope? Von Franz writes that "when Jung's students once asked him if the third (and probably most horrendous) world war could be avoided, he answered that it depended on how many individuals could reconcile the opposites within themselves."[2]

Without developing the capacity to see and integrate shadow, we stand to destroy ourselves *and* our ideals; what awareness each individual can develop may save us, for we each can contribute our share toward a critical mass of awareness that is building in our world. "The only devils in the world," said Mahatma Gandhi, who understood the power of individual action, "are those running around in our own hearts. That is where the battle should be fought."

In the process of adapting to civilization, we inevitably come face-to-face with emotions and desires which society says are either taboo or "uncivilized." The average person, believing that he or she is no more than their ego-identity, represses these unacceptable aspects to the unconscious where they coalesce into a more or less autonomous splinter-personality: it is all shadow. The more strongly and rigidly we identify with our "I," the more we must deny the other aspects of our personality. Such adaptation comes at a great cost to the individual soul: what we cannot admit in ourselves, we are condemned to experience fatefully in others. The concealment of those unacceptable parts, and the posturing required to hide what we cannot love in ourselves, steals energy that is then otherwise unavailable to us.

So we can't really live our lives fully without dealing with the shadow. The shadow is the thing that constricts, the narrow gate; until you find enough courage ("take heart") to own *all* of your experience and confront your personal demons, your aliveness will be greatly limited. We each must confront our fear and shame, and recover those parts of ourselves that have been demonized or exiled from our conscious awareness. What follows is the moral effort of shadow work; through discernment, we find a place in our consciousness for what previously has been denied.

The social standards of our culture tend to discourage this expansion of awareness. One becomes "well-adjusted" at the expense of personal truth. To get to our personal truth we have to suffer, to actually feel such un-love and torment that we recognize our suffering and realize that something is missing. When the point of recognition arrives—if it arrives— what we've banished from consciousness rises to the surface and becomes a moral problem: we start to recognize our own dark nature as real and present. We've now entered what Jung himself called "the essential condition for self-knowledge."[3] Shadow work can yield dramatic results, a new humility accompanied by an increase in energetic aliveness, a newfound compassion for oneself and others, and, for some, an initiation and a rebirth. As the ancient oracular verses of the *I Ching* express it:

It is only when we have the courage to face things
exactly as they are,
without any self-deception or illusion,
that a light will develop out of events,
by which the path to success may be recognized.[4]

The moral effort of shadowwork is enhanced if we can "name the figures in our garden." By personifying our shadow with language we grant reality to these disowned energies. Most spiritual traditions have long-standing practices for naming the shadow qualities. In his book, *A Path with Heart*, meditation teacher Jack Kornfield details these contemplative techniques of naming the demons: the Sufis identify their difficult aspects as *Nafs*; Christian contemplatives differentiate a host of demons, assigning them with various levels of power; Buddhist practitioners of "skillful means" personify the negative energetic emanations of mind as "Hindrances to Clarity," symbolizing them as manifestations of Mara, the God of Darkness. According to Kornfield, giving names to our grasping and our wanting, our angers and our fears, our boredom and our judgments, our restlessness and our doubt, expands our understanding, compassion, and freedom. We can take the manure of experience and use it as fertilizer for enlightenment.

"Whether difficulties or pleasures," Kornfield writes, "the naming of our experience is the first step in bringing them to a wakeful conscious attention. Mindfully naming and acknowledging our experience allows us to investigate our life, to inquire into whatever aspect or problem of life presents itself to us . . . as we clearly sense and name our experience, we can notice what brings it about and how we can respond to it more fully and skillfully."[5]

The modern psychotherapist in his or her role as mysta-
gogue or psychopomp—guiding souls through initiation and
transition—is uniquely suited to the task of shadowwork in
American culture. This specialized process almost always
begins in a confessional mode: the therapist provides the container of human relationship while the client addresses the
unconscious sources of his or her suffering. The two undertake
a dialogue, an often painstaking procedure of self-awareness,
through which a third awareness can eventually emerge, a synthesis that (hopefully) affects both parties.

This third awareness has enabling possibilities for embodying the shadow, for the redemption of those parts we have
rejected or projected onto others. Though this is not always
the intention or the result of the psychotherapeutic process, it
is potentially the most important of outcomes. With the help of
the therapist, we develop the psychological skills needed to
continually bring the shadow to consciousness, to see both our
constructive and destructive capacities, and to own our share
of human imperfection.

Patricia Berry, the author of the following essay, "Light and
Shadow," combines the skills of a seasoned psychotherapist (a
Zürich-trained Jungian analyst) with the straightforwardness
of a midwestern American. Speaking from her own experience
with shadow awareness, she qualifies the advantages and the
limitations of the psychotherapeutic—and especially the
Jungian therapeutic—sensibility.

—J. A.

Light and Shadow

PATRICIA BERRY

ALL MY PROFESSIONAL TRAINING and, until recently, most of my professional life, has been in the Jungian world. I was 23 when I went to Zürich. I had been in therapy for several years and had gotten the idea I might become a therapist too. This therapy had been mostly supportive, and not profoundly deep—no doubt because I wasn't either. However, the work I did was enough to make me realize that before I started working as a therapist, I'd better get myself looked into more thoroughly. Jungian analysis seemed a good choice for this since it dealt with dreams and the unconscious. So I went to Jung's Zürich and for 12 years immersed myself in depth analysis.

The analysis, however, was not the only valuable part of this experience; living in Zürich was at least as important. As a foreigner, I became painfully aware of my American identity. At that time, Americans were considered by most Europeans to be naive, unbounded, unrefined, imperialistic oafs. I discovered that when I was simply being myself, my more cultivated, European friends and acquaintances looked upon me as childish and unsophisticated. For example, I knew little about food culture and nothing about wine. This was in the 1960s when most American wine still came in screw-top bottles. My clothes were characteristically American—boxy, if I dressed up, Earth Mother gingham if I didn't. In this country where even laborers dressed fashionably, I was completely without style, devoid of the cosmopolitan elegance of even the simplest Zürich citizen.

On Sundays the Swiss would gather their families and, clothed in suits and ties and nice dresses, go for walks. You didn't work on Sunday, or even wash your car or vacuum the house. Sunday was clearly a time for parading, perhaps stopping for coffee or a wienerli at an outdoor cafe. Very civilized.

I tried hard to adapt to this more sophisticated culture. I threw out my pedal-pushers, my madras plaids, my flowing hippie stuff, my blue jeans, and changed my hair from '60s "mess" to a more stylish European cut. I learned to stroll on Sunday and to buy groceries ahead of time, since no shops would be open on Sundays or holidays. For my pragmatic American mind, it was a mystery how Swiss shops and businesses could survive. At the time, there were no fast food franchises in Switzerland—no Burger King or McDonalds— where you could eat the same food over and over again, safely certain that nothing would vary. Further, I didn't understand how so many people—a whole culture—could manage not being able to go to the store whenever they chose. This lack of convenience and necessary delay of gratification required quite an adjustment for me. Though I adapted as best I could, I never overcame my sense of myself as a naive American.

A certain lack of cultural refinement—awkwardness with formality and structure—seemed to reside in my very bones. My American shadow was me.

I hadn't seen this shadow before going to Europe. I hadn't possessed the perspective from which to see it. Up until then who I was just seemed "normal." It was my first realization that to see shadow requires a separate vantage point from which to observe it—as well as a source of light to project it. Until then it was as if I could not see my shadow because I was standing in the middle of it, the way we stand in our own shadow on a sunny day at high noon.

To see the shadow, there needs to be a contrasting point of view, one that allows us to discover that our values and behavior—particularly those we have assimilated culturally, and which we generally take for granted—aren't just objective responses to the world but are expressions of who we are.

I also discovered at this time that when we truly do encounter the shadow, and start working with it consciously, it can feel like a loss of identity. We can no longer naively continue to "be ourselves." Indeed, during my years in Zürich, there was no way I could any longer take myself and my point of view for granted. I became "self conscious." I paid attention to my every move, and nothing came "naturally" anymore. Literally and figuratively, I was stumbling over my own shadow.

Jung once characterized the ego (by which he meant one's sense of oneself) as the most unconscious part of the personality. He meant because we are so identified with it, the ego becomes virtually invisible to us. After all, how could one see what you are one with? In my experience, the loss of identity that comes by standing outside yourself marks the beginnings of shadow awareness.

One should, of course, make a distinction between being self-critical and becoming aware of one's shadow. It is easy to say, for example, that I'm lazy, clumsy, or selfish. And these certainly can be aspects of the shadow. But it's not the difficult part of shadow awareness. What's difficult to acknowledge is that with which we are thoroughly identitified—who I think I am. When this deep sense of identity is questioned, shadow awareness truly begins. And it can feel quite horrible. We become less sure of ourselves, less embodied, less comfortable.

When I began going through this in Zürich (I'm still going through it, of course, but I'm used to it now), I felt absolutely decimated.

To See the Shadow
We Must Look at the Light

SINCE SHADOW WORK DOES BRING ON this uncomfortable sense of losing one's identity, the second vantage point which allows us to look at ourselves, and which provides the "light," is a critical factor. Think of it this way: a shadow cannot exist on its own. There must be at least two other elements involved: 1) a light; and 2) an object which blocks the light. When I went to Zürich, the Swiss values I became so acutely aware of provided the light; the object blocking the light comprised the cultural values I had brought with me as an American.

It is important to understand that the shadow, as I'm using the term in this article, does not accurately depict the object from which it is cast, any more than the shadow cast as we walk down the street in the afternoon accurately depicts the shape and size of our physical bodies. On the contrary, the shadow will be distorted according to the position of the sun in relation to our body. At five o'clock, our shadow will be longer than our body is tall; at one o'clock, it will be shorter, and so forth.

Because of the important part played by the light, or (following the analogy) by the nature of the second vantage point that allows us to see our "shadow self," we cannot fully understand our shadow unless we also familiarize ourselves with the light.

As individuals doing shadow work, we are usually using the therapist as our outside vantage point, our light and our eyes into ourselves. That "source of light" which the therapist represents, will clearly have an effect on the shadow we see. For that reason, if no other, we cannot take this light source for granted any more than we can take our own egos for granted. One obvious distortion that might occur has to do with the therapeutic methods themselves. Much of what the professional psychology journals call shadow work is not only not shadow work but is frequently in serious conflict with it. For example, in working psychotherapeutically and supportively— common techniques taught in most college programs for marriage and family counselors, as well as clinical psychologists— one's efforts are generally directed toward "self-affirmation," that is, helping the client more firmly establish, enrich, and "fill out" a sense of self-identity and self-worth based on who they are right now. The goal is to empower the ego, to teach the client to say, in effect, "it's okay to be me." In many cases, the therapist makes little or no effort to help the client develop a deeper self awareness. There is no effort to increase the person's awareness of their ego and how it shapes their daily choices and expressions.

Shadow work, rather than automatically taking the "it's-okay-to-be-me" stance, requires that we first explore and identify the self we are now. Rather than arbitrarily affirming that self from the start, the initial stages of shadow work ask us first to know what we're affirming. As a result, we may very well find ourselves less empowered, more split or divided inside, less sure of ourselves. We are, by necessity, dis-identifying with the self we have known; we are establishing a certain distance from it, and thus feeling "less ourselves." We begin to feel that there is more going on, both inside and outside ourselves, than we ever imagined. Ultimately, what we affirm or don't affirm about ourselves becomes a selective process, based on increased knowledge of who we are.

Multiple Personalities of the Psyche

ANOTHER AREA WHERE CURRENT PSYCHOTHERAPY may be in conflict with shadow work is in the treatment and discussion of "multiple personalities." Jung himself believed that the psyche is multiple, dissociable, composed of relatively autonomous figures, complexes, or partly developed personalities. I often wonder if much of today's talk about "multiple personality disorder" isn't a distorted view of what are actually normal manifestations of these various aspects of the self.

As we look more closely at the complex structure of the self, we discover that what Jung describes as "ego" is not necessarily the most developed part of the psyche. In his work with the patient he called "SW," for example, he discovered that the ego personality was silly and adolescent, while one of the other personalities, one of her shadows (Ivene), seemed mature, worldly wise, and of much broader vision. Given this observation, we need to ask what aspect of the self are we supporting when we arbitrarily set up psychotherapeutic goals that "it's okay to be me"?

Control and the Mysteries
of the Unconscious

ANOTHER CATCHWORD WE FIND IN CONTEMPORARY SOCIETY, both popular and professional, is the concept of being in control. It is generally felt that being in control is good, while being out of control is bad. From a broader perspective, we know that being in control is at best something of an illusion. In any case, it is the ego that seeks and highly values this illusion. Indeed, such emphasis on control really bespeaks how out of control many of us feel. It is an expression of the ego trying to impose its own values upon the world, seeking security and a release from fears the ego itself has created by forcing the world into that ego's own image and likeness.

The quest for control—all-or-nothing, black-and-white logic—is characteristic of the compulsive thought patterns of the addictive personality. What's more, that same quest for control keeps addictive people thinking and experiencing their lives addictively. There is no way to get outside ourselves, to establish the perspective necessary for viewing our shadows, as long as we cling to this thought pattern. According to Jung, the ego's illusions of control can use some softening, some dissolving of either-or, black-and-white thinking. Indeed, this is ultimately what shadow awareness accomplishes for us, allowing us to see that there is much more to life than what the ego would like to see.

From a Jungian point of view, it is always the unconscious that is most interesting. In its aims and activities the unconscious is of interest because it is much more than what we know, understand, and can control. The mysteries it contains fill out the personality, making it richer, more complex and, ultimately, more flexible—all in all, more able to adapt and solve the problems of living. I like to think of the ego in its more appropriate role as a kind of stage manager or housekeeper, organizing, picking up the scattered pieces, tying up loose ends, if only temporarily, just for the sake of efficiency.

There can be little doubt that if we regard the ego, as Jung did, as the most unconscious part of the personality—what we take most for granted—it would appear that much of what we may create in psychotherapy may be little more than better housekeepers. And in the process, we are creating an increasingly vast unconsciousness, the reservoir of inner drives that pull our strings, actually increasing that sense of our lives being "out of control." I think it is necessary to look at the very real possibility that self-affirmation, self-identity, control, and empowerment may be part of the problem rather than the solution.

Cultural Shadows, Cultural Lights

AT THE STONE CENTER in Wellesley, Massachusetts, a number of women scholars (Carol Gilligan, Jean Baker Miller, and others) have done detailed research into our current psychological theories. This research is important to us in terms of our present discussion because it reveals a cultural bias, and a portion of our cultural shadow, that might otherwise remain quite invisible to us. This research shines a light on how our notions of child development (and self-development) reflect, in a mostly unconscious way, cultural values such as autonomy, independence, self-sufficiency, achievement, initiative, and individualism, while other values such as the development of empathy and relatedness are all but neglected.

The researchers at the Stone Center have been able to show that relational development, that is, the ability to think in terms of and relate with others, is given little importance. We're not talking about pop psychology here; rather, the observations at the Stone Center are about the more serious and carefully thought out theories from which most of today's psychologists draw their knowledge and expertise, and from which they draw significant aspects of their therapeutic goals. Instead of emphasizing how to relate with others, the focus in most developmental psychology theory has been, and is continuing to be, on the achievement of personal autonomy—the ability to be independent and self-sufficient, to have initiative, and, of course, to achieve.

The Stone Center is feminist in orientation, so part of their aim is to reveal gender differences—how little girls are encouraged to develop more in the area of relationship values, while boys are encouraged to be more autonomous. When we look at this research, we begin to ask what human development would look like if we adopted empathy and relatedness as primary goals or values. I would imagine that we would tend to develop the ability to listen, to "witness" without the need to offer opinions, arguments, or "solutions." We might become better able to maintain openness and hear each other out without prematurely imposing judgment. Mutuality rather than hierarchy would be emphasized, fostering back and forth discussions without one party having to seek dominance over others. The ability to play different roles—from dominant-submissive to submissive-dominant with fluidity would reflect a high degree of relatedness. By developing relatedness values, we would gain the ability to suspend our personal autonomy, to stand outside ourselves to better appreciate other perspectives. And, of course, the moment we are able to entertain these other perspectives, we become better able to see our shadows.

Let me offer yet another perspective, another source of light, if you will. I went to Japan a few years ago, where I attended a conference on child rearing. We in the West imagine that when children are born into the world, they are deeply connected or "fused" with the mother. Given that perspective, we look upon their development as the child's increasing separation from the mother, ultimately leading to its autonomy. For the Japanese, however, the child arrives as a stranger in the world. In its natural state it is viewed as unrelated and selfish. The goal in Japanese child rearing, in contrast to the goals of the West, is to help the individual develop relational skills. The educational work is to weave the child's natural individuality into larger and more extensive relational contexts: from self (as in selfishness), to family, to school, to place of work, to empire, to world, and so forth.

While I was in Japan, I also went to see Kabuki theater and the No play, where the highest paid actor is "the invisibile one," who artfully slips around the stage, arranging the garments of other actors and moving props in and out. That figure is in many ways symbolic of the positive aspects of the Japanese developmental goals—to develop personal characteristics of serving the needs of others without drawing attention to one's self.

As viewed from the perspective of the American developmental model, the Japanese goals might be seen as leading to a conformity which seems nothing short of ridiculous—and somewhat threatening—to the American mind. We may see it as leading to the kind of "self-sacrifice" we saw in kamikaze pilots during WWII, which, cast in the light of the American vantage point, produces the shadow of the Japanese cultural perspective.

When we take a look at other ways of imagining psychological development, we see that the possibilities are nearly limitless. And in the light of any of these other vantage points we might better see the shadows of our own psychological perspectives. The more we see of other cultures the more we become aware of how much emphasis we place on individuality. We see why it is that we give so much attention to themes such as fusing and merging, or, by contrast, separation and individuation. We begin to see that within this developmental model, we are always going back and forth between the two poles, caught up in a kind of compulsive or addictive logic; if we're not autonomous, we must be merging. This either-or thinking powerfully increases the effect of the shadow self on our daily lives and on the national psyche.

Recognizing How Ideals Project Shadows

ONE OF THE CURRENT SHADOWS cast by our Western notions of individuality and independence is called "codependence." It stands to reason that if our developmental theories placed inordinately high values on independence and individuality, it would logically lead to viewing too much relatedness as a disease. I'm not arguing that unhealthy codependency does not exist, any more than I intend to argue that multiple personality disorder does not exist or that there are not legitimate self-affirmation issues. It's just that how we see these issues, that is, what we make of them, is based on a perspective that in large part is established by the developmental theories with which we are aligned. Those theories make up the light source that determines the shape and size of the shadow.

Let me go back for a moment and borrow from my experiences in Switzerland. In Zürich, I saw myself as an ugly American because I had momentarily stepped into the light of the European perspective—or at least what I imagined to be the European perspective. From this vantage point I could see myself as an ugly American. But that particular shadow was a product not only of my culturally assimilated American values, which up to then had remained fairly invisible to me, but also of the position of the light offered by the European perspective.

It is the same with our developmental theories: as Westerners, our light is individuality and autonomy. Merging, fusion, and joining are interpreted as the shadows cast by that light. We take the position that children should outgrow fused relationships and become independent. If they don't, we define them as codependent, and that's bad. That's the shadow.

But we can shift the light and get a slightly different shadow. If I stand in Zürich and view my European neighbors from my American perspective, I see them as stilted, overstructured, inefficient, nonproductive (or, at least, not as productive as they could be). The children, though quiet and well-behaved, aren't as emotionally free and creative as we believe our American children to be.

Let's try shifting the light again, seeing the shadow take on still another form. Let's imagine that in this case we are placing a high value on fusing, merging, and dependence, or mutual interdependence. Autonomy would begin to be viewed as the shadow—let us call it "the Lone Wolf Syndrome." In this light, the clear-eyed, young, visionary pioneer, wandering unfettered off across the plains—Davy Crockett, Daniel Boone, Jim Bowie, the Lone Ranger—all begin to look like psychopaths. What were heroes in the light of the independence-autonomy model suddenly become shadow. Can you imagine how the Japanese might view these characters? As terrifying and "insane" as the kamikaze pilot might be to us, these heroes of automony must seem quite berserk, though perhaps fascinating, to them!

So we begin to learn about our shadow and the assumptions we make about the world when we momentarily take the position of another vantage point, another perspective.

Shadows Within the Shadows of Childhood

IN RECENT YEARS, THERE HAS BEEN INCREASED INTEREST in the child and childhood. In a very real way, we can say this is the era of the child. Adults are now labeled "adult children" when found to be victims of dysfunctional or pathological family situations. The prevalent image is of the child as victim—abused, powerless, the Rousseauian innocent. The present perspective is that if problems exist for the child, it is not by virtue of his or her own nature, painted as innocent, pure, and loving. Rather, the child's misfortunes and wounds are seen as events to which he or she has been subjected through coercion, overt abuse, lack of love, or sheer indifference.

Freud's view of the child was very different. He saw the child as polymorphous perverse, omnipotent with desire, driven by the libidinous impulses of the id. He saw the child not as a victim of outer forces over which it had no influence or control, but as a being wrestling with an internal world of innate conflict.

Jung's child is similar to Freud's, not wholly a victim of its environment by any means. Jung's child had help from many sources, the archetypes of the collective unconscious, for example, providing alternatives to even the most dysfunctional family situations.

Certainly our present Rousseauian model of the child, as well as Freud's and Jung's models, all portray important aspects of the child archetype. Indeed, most would agree that the child is libidinous, omnipotent, and innocent, as well as victimized, imaginative, and creative. But the aspects presently shouting for attention in our society focus on seeing the child as victim. It's as though the time has come for us to look more closely at this victim aspect of the child. It screams to us, "See me. I am a victim. I am abused. I am powerless. See me!"

We have little choice but to see and hear. This cry is the cry of an aspect of the child that has been collectively repressed for a very long time. At last it is speaking out. What was once hidden in the shadows is now coming to light. One might object to the focus on the child's victimization. Of course, one might wish to broaden the light to include more of the child, to argue, for example, that child abuse is by no means new.

In 1991, the *Journal of Psychohistory* devoted its fall issue to the issue of child abuse. The lead article argued that child abuse is not more frequent now than in the past; in fact, it is probably less frequent. Lloyd Demause, the author of this article, contends that the incest taboo is not universal; rather, what is universal is incest itself—a statement which challenges both Freud and Jung, who assumed the incest taboo to be universal. Historically, Demause claims that though incestuous marriage has always been prohibited, sexual contact among family members has not.

Demause cites incestuous practices that are still sanctioned or tolerated in various societies and subcultures even now. Most of his examples come from the Middle and Far East. Based on this material, it appears that what we are now calling sexual abuse was always there but wasn't perceived or perhaps even experienced as abuse. Even so, within the context of the shadow, we need to ask why the issue of childhood sexual abuse is emerging now. Why it has come to light we can only speculate. But as with many issues around the shadow, it is perhaps emerging because it is now ready to be dealt with.

From a Jungian perspective, we can also look at our present emphasis on the child from a different vantage point: What is the shadow of this new model of the child? How does it distort what we see? What does it leave out? In our eagerness to address the issues of the helpless child, the child as innocent victim, we should not forget that this current figure is but a single piece of the child archetype. What about the other parts—the child as self-indulgent, deceitful, creative, resourceful, omnipotent, imaginative, tyrannical? These, too, exist. Remember the Salem witch trials were triggered by two little girls who spread the rumor that someone was a witch. Fueled by a culture with a long history of anti-witch sentiment, this rumor became contagious, resulting in the burning of many people who were guilty of no crime whatsoever.

The Dangers of Collective Movements

ANOTHER DIFFICULTY THAT COMES UP FOR ME AS a Jungian in dealing with the child as victim is the realization that we are dealing with the expression of a collective movement. The Jungian emphasis is on individuation. At the same time, I must say, we are deeply concerned with issues such as universal archetypes, symbols, and the collective unconscious, from which the person individuates.

Because the contemporary victimized child identifies with only one portion of the archetype, there is a splitting, or fragmentation, in which a portion of the child shadow is projected elsewhere—onto parents, other family members, and so forth. The child as victim sets the stage for the individual to deny blame or responsibility for what has occurred, treating that blame or responsibility as if it were all out there. Another difficulty is that insofar as this identification with the victimized child is a collective contagion, it has become a mass movement that is an unconscious force in the culture. Given Jung's warnings, it is potentially dangerous, as is any mass movement of this kind.

As we deal with the issue of unconscious mass movements, it is impossible to ignore the cultural events that Jung himself witnessed in his time. He witnessed some of the most frightening expresssions of collective forces in history, in the form of Nazi Germany and the spread of Fascism. So Jung was particularly aware of the shadow of collective movements and the unconscious herd phenomenon that accompanies them.

Make no mistake. My urgency about looking at the whole child archetype rather than fragmenting it and focusing only on the victimized child, should in no way be construed as implying that contemporary issues of child victimization should not be taken seriously. On the contrary! But we need to go further. We need to perhaps look at the victimized child as a repressed aspect of our culture itself. Long held in the unconscious, that portion of the child has been hidden in the shadow, with portions of our society denying the victim in ourselves and projecting it outward for others in our society to take on. This possibility, of course, suggests that the emergence of the child as victim brings up complex issues that must be addressed both culturally and individually.

Are Symptoms Alone Proof Enough for the Psyche?

A QUESTION OF GREAT CONCERN FOR VICTIMS OF SEXUAL ABUSE is whether or not the abuse occurred in fact. To my mind, this matters less than what the person is experiencing psychologically, since I believe that visions, dreams, fantasies, and active imagination are indeed real and that they "create reality every day," as Jung says. However, most people in our culture do not have this attitude. For most, it makes a great difference whether something is factual or whether it exists *only* at an emotional level. So, these people go to great lengths trying to remember what actually happened so that they can separate fact from fiction.

I believe that when we are working with the shadow, we need to deal with the psychological reality as such—regardless of the external facts. And in the process of doing so, we need to be cautious of the vantage point from which we are viewing this situation. For example, Claudia Black counsels that if you have the personality traits and defenses associated with one who has been abused—low self-esteem, difficulty trusting, a tendency to dissociate, and so on—then it is safe to assume that you have been abused. The problem with this and other categorical thinking of this kind, is that if we look from the right vantage, we all seem to fit the mold; we all tend to have low self-esteem, difficulty trusting, and a tendency to dissociate at least some of the time. But does that literally mean that we've been sexually abused as children? Evidence would seem to indicate otherwise.

Nevertheless, I believe that sexual contact between adults and children is quite common, perhaps common enough that we do not need to spend a lot of time in therapy deciding whether or not it has occurred. Thus, I frequently find myself saying—or at least thinking—"Okay, let's assume it did occur and go on from there. Let's explore its impact *on you*." If my tone betrays that I have any doubt about the event being true, then we're in for another round of did it or didn't it "really happen," which to my way of thinking is a waste of time.

However, the question must be treated delicately. It's as if the child victim in all of us requires a direct and literal response in order to ground his or her emotions and make them "real." The child easily loses its connection to emotion, gets distracted, forgets, adapts. To hold an emotion over time, consciously and consistently, is a developmental achievement. Nobody does all the time. So, the child in us may need help holding its connection to emotion. The child asks for certainty, not ambiguity. It asks for stability, fixity, safety, not the double entendres and contradictions that we juggle in adult life. And, let's remember, this child exists in all of us, regardless of how mature we might like to think we are.

My own inner child is the dumb one, the one who doesn't get the joke, doesn't make the turn, or the shy one who clings to her mother's skirts, never dares venture forth until she knows what's what. The literal assures this child of what's what. At the same time that we employ the literal for this sense of security, we cannot forget that the literal is also an illusion. There is no mother there in the psyche, really, no stability, no safety. The mother the child sees is never exactly the mother that is, but rather a mental fabrication of that mother. But the illusion is important, even for the adult mind, with all its sophistication. Just as the child needs to come and go from the mother, we seem to need fixed points—basic assumptions, propositions, givens—which we can count on, if only fleetingly, before venturing forth, spinning our theories, trying out new attitudes. And we often need to invent these fixed points in order to have the illusions of safety, even when we might know they are our own inventions.

Body Awareness and the Literal

ANOTHER ASPECT OF THE CHILD'S NEED FOR THE LITERAL has to do with the body, with the sense of one's self as a concrete organism, living, breathing, feeling, and moving. The abused child, we must note, dissociates from its pain and thus from its body, thereafter finding it difficult to relate to itself in an "embodied" way. Its sense of its body is numbed by the pain of the damage that's been inflicted. So, when that person relives the abusive experience, he or she not only experiences the abuse again but experiences the body as such, his or her concreteness.

In a very real way, the awareness of body that I'm suggesting here is an awareness gained by mortification, through suffering. The implication in shadow work may be that it can be important to imagine things as being even more literal than might be the case. We need to use our imaginations to relive the experience of abuse that has become a psychic reality—whether or not it was a physical reality.

Earlier I said that shadow awareness had to do with the ability to shift our vantage point, to put the ego in perspective, to loosen the sense of identity. If I seem to be proposing something to the contrary, it is because shadow awareness also has a shadow. Let me elaborate.

In the process of gaining shadow awareness, the work is indeed to disidentify, which can be very difficult and painful. Once this is accomplished, however, and we have brought the shadow into the light, we tend to reject the shadow and identify with the source of light that has allowed us to see the shadow. Thus, once I was able to see my American shadow when I was living in Zürich, I disidentified with it and identified instead with the European perspective that had allowed me to see that earlier shadow. To do this is essential, allowing us to get a better look at our shadow. But it isn't the end of the process. The next step is to reconnect with the shadow we've just left and try to understand it, give it credit, look for the value in it. This is what Jung meant when he spoke of the gold in the shit. It takes work to go back and find this gold.

Literalization and Symbols

WHEN DEALING WITH THE VICTIMIZED CHILD SHADOW, I use literalization as a tool. By this I mean I may, for example, ask leading, reductive questions aimed at simplifying and intensifying the person's identification with the experience of abuse. Who abused you? Can you describe exactly what happened? What was said or not said? What was felt, seen, heard? I'll work to pull out as many feelings as possible around the abuse, and explore how these feelings reverberate in the present for that person.

Barbara Walters, the journalist, is brilliant with her use of the kind of literalism I'm describing here. She beams in on people with direct, reductive questions: How did you feel when you saw your child run over by a truck? Were you sad when your father died? What did you feel at the breakup of your marriage? What did you do at the loss of your career? She asks intrusively, but she gets excellent, interesting answers.

Literalistic interviewing of this kind goes straight to the child. And the child in us responds with its own condensed, non-subtle and highly concretized emotions.

Another characteristic of the child that is emerging in our culture at this time is that it does not exist alone. Culturally, this is a time of relationship. Things exist in relation with other things. The child develops in relation with objects and as a part of various systems, particularly the family system. In family systems theory, every individual is dependent on, and related to, every other individual within the system. One is born into a family with the urge, the instinct, let's say, to serve the system. There is an innate love not only for one's parents but for one's siblings and the system itself—even if serving this love requires an eating disorder, addiction, or psychosis.

Jung's view of the family is, as one might suspect, quite different. Rather than an interdependent whole, he sees the family as a collection of individuals who may, at various times, merge or move into what he calls *participation mystique*. But each individual has unique challenges, myths, and destinies to work out—assuming they are marked for individuation, to *be* unique individuals, beyond the collective herd.

A Splitting of the Shadow

THERE IS A TENDENCY IN ALL OF US to take even the theory we embrace (especially the theory we embrace) and turn it into a defense to justify our weaknesses and thus avoid anything that might be personally difficult or threatening. That may be the case with our Jungian emphasis on individuation. When the shadow takes hold of individuation, we get a splitting, and an antipathy, creating hierarchies. The individual becomes of higher importance than the collective; the unique rises above the familial, the archetype above the common, the special above the ordinary.

We have to look at the aspect of the child that has been dominant in Jungian psychology—that is the "special" child, the heroic child with partly divine parentage (one parent is God). That child is typically born in lowly, difficult circumstances. But because of his specialness (his secret, archetypal lineage), he is destined to achieve far beyond his lowly birth and surroundings. There are a number of possible ends to this myth. The hero might bring back to the culture the fruits of his labors; or he might be destroyed by the collective forces, the other gods from which he has been alienated as a result of his struggles.

The kind of child currently asserting its voice in the collective is of a different sort—not one that leaves its parents for the sake of more spiritually transformative or soul-connected forces. Rather, it clings to the connection with its actual parents, no matter how bad they were. In fact, because they were so bad, this child expends huge efforts to remember and relive the wrongs it perceives as being perpetrated—which, as I've noted earlier, is a stage of its healing. My point here is that this child *insists* on being related and insists on suffering its relationship to its actual parents and the concrete, traumatic, literal situations to which it was exposed.

I think this child has something to teach us Jungians. Whereas our child has been divine, its shadow perhaps effete, special, and isolationist, the contemporary child is demanding, embroiled, simplistic, blaming, living its shadow, and adamantly relational in the process. I believe it is the shadow of our Jungian child that has led so many of us into the self-contained domain of our highly individualized practices. The image that comes to mind is of the isolated analyst in a kind of therapeutic "ivory tower," narcissistically (though innocently and unconsciously) living out power needs in the shelter of this isolation.

As we address issues of working with the shadows of both our own systems and our analysands, many of us in Jungian psychology are learning a lot about boundaries and ethics. We didn't used to talk about such things. I had never even heard the word "boundaries" until after I returned to the States twelve years ago. To a large part, it's become a widely recognized issue because of the modern child we are now finding in this culture—a child who speaks up, demanding safety, protection, and containment. This child blows the whistle on what it considers abusive. My own (inner) child didn't do that; it didn't even feel it was being or had been abused.

The child in ourselves was the child of a very different myth. What if Christ had felt abused, or Moses, or Oedipus, or Hercules? If they had tried to "work it through" with their parents, they would have never gotten on with the story. Same with us. We felt the necessity to move on, to transform, to move beyond our experiences of abuse. We developed, in part, by learning how to handle the peculiarities and weaknesses of our analysts. We didn't concern ourselves with how their shadows affected us.

The child in the patient who enters analysis nowadays is quite different. It exists not only, as we've said, in relation with living members of a family, but its problems may also be echoing relations with earlier generations—an interesting variation on Jung's early notion of a racial unconscious.

In any case, family, however longitudinally extended, is the problem—the dysfunctional family. So, not only is this child radically related to family, it is radically related to addictive substances and activities. Addiction, as you know, is construed quite broadly nowadays. One can be addicted not only to drugs, alcohol, gambling (those were the old addictions) but now also to food, sex, relationship, work, love, activity, even novelty. Judging from the current literature, virtually any human activity, undertaken immoderately, can become an addiction.

If we come from families in which any member was addicted in any of these ways, we are called "adult children." So, the child and addiction are closely related. If we aren't addicted ourselves (which we probably are, given the range of possibilities) someone else in our family or extended family is or has been. But even then, even if we can't find anybody—if we have problems, we've obviously come from a dysfunctional family, and that's the same thing. Given this tautalogical tangle, it's safe to assume that we're all "adult children" for whom addiction, in some form, figures into our psychologies.

For addiction there is therapy—the most pervasive form being 12-step programs. It has been obvious to me from the meetings I've attended that what is being worked on, however, is not only the addiction (though that's the presenting complaint, that's why people go) but also relationship itself. This aspect of the therapy is accomplished through an elaborate set of rules and conventions operative during the meeting.

Persons are not to interrupt or to ask questions, make comments, or in any way to engage someone who is speaking. There is no "cross-talk" (which is to say, no normal interaction). Rather, each person speaks of their own struggles, their own sufferings, or whatever, from as deep a level as they are able/willing, and then that's simply left, that simply is.

The result of this process is that a new level of connection among persons is created indirectly, a joining by way of the commonality, the humanity, of suffering itself. What is overly personal for a child in a bind with his or her parental images becomes an impersonal sense of connection through suffering—an *unus mundus* based on the commonality (perhaps even the universality) of despair. What I'm saying is that within the collective culture itself there is a therapeutic form, these 12-step programs, which, imagined alchemically, seen finalistically, are addressing and transforming the dilemma of the overly relational, traumatized, literalizing child of our time. I suppose what functions as the transformational symbol here is the "higher power" that is spoken of; the higher power (or the transformational powers of the Self), born out of both a very personal and literal suffering is at once superordinant, beyond any merely personal life.

The Future of Jungian Psychology

WHEN WE ASK THE QUESTION of how Jungian perspectives might serve the psychotherapeutic movements of contemporary society, we get some interesting answers. Unlike many of the psychotherapies of recent times, the Jungian psychology offers a sophisticated and subtle set of awarenesses based upon a substantial history and tradition.

Above all, *Jungian psychology knows a great deal about shadow*. It knows, unlike many more mainstream psychologies, that everything that exists, every movement, attitude, person, stance (its own psychology included) exists with a shadow. And not just one shadow but many! The Jungian attitude teaches us to bring shadow awareness into every situation we view.

The task is to look to our own shadows. But we must go further. What we really need is an awareness of the shadow of shadow awareness, a deeper knowledge of the shadow of the shadow. As a Jungian, I think that all of us in the helping professions ought to be engaged in that pursuit.

PART III

Between Masculine and Feminine

Introduction

You yourself are a conflict that rages
in itself and against itself,
in order to melt its incompatible substances,
the male and the female, in the fire of suffering.

—C. G. Jung

THE BATTLE OF THE SEXES RAGES ON. American men
and women continue to hash out their differences in public and in private, searching for the new paradigm of relationship and balance. All areas of contemporary life—the workplace, the home, institutions—are affected by the shifting
status quo between men and women. And it seems increasingly
difficult for the dialogue between the sexes to be a constructive
one. We have movements for men and movements for women;
movements that run the gamut from free-love advocates and
romantics to misogynists and man-haters.

Since the rise of a more strident feminism in the early
1970s, which instigated a more public dialogue about the roles
of men and women in American society, there has been a collective paranoia growing on the periphery of the culture. To
state it simply, it seems that men have projected their worst
castration fears onto women; women have blamed the domi-
nance/victim cycle on men. The only safe conclusion to be
drawn from this stage of engagement between the sexes might

be that all relationships, by necessity, begin with and consist of an enormous amount of projection. Though there is usually an apparent justification for our projections—a "hook"—they often tell more about us than the other person. In the case of collective projections, we are looking at a pernicious process of enemy-making that resolves nothing and hurts many. We must not be lulled into thinking that, even if we withdraw our projections, the contents of the projections evaporate. There is a moral task for all men and women in America to discuss the fair, appropriate, and flexible ways we can be together in the world.

At the present time we do not have a collective agreement about masculine and feminine roles, about gender attitudes and behaviors. In the cultural vanguard, we find women who are tending toward action and recognition in the outer world and men who are seeking their deeper personal truths. As men and women experiment with formerly polarized sex roles and the "prison of gender," we are all challenged to understand our true natures, as distinct from what our society has expected of us.

According to June Singer, the psychoanalyst and author, there are two growing tendencies among American men and women:

> The first I perceive as an attempt to obliterate the cultural and sociological differences between masculine and feminine functioning in the workaday world. This I call the tendency toward androgyny. The second tendency appears to be a resistance against the first! One part of the population seems intent upon achieving as complete an integration . . . as possible, by educating people away from stereotypical sex attitudes and by providing equal opportunity and responsibility for both sexes in all areas. The other part of the population seems intent upon thwarting this integration by insisting upon the essential differences

between male and female consciousness and upon the necessity to conform attitudes and behavior to these differences.[1]

As this process has been cooking in the culture over the past 25 years, we have not found a place of meeting between these opposites. It may be optimistic to think we can or will.

The old relationship paradigm in American life, the nuclear family, seems to have lost its footing. Meanwhile, we all bemoan the decline of the extended family. Today, even the nuclear family is revealed as a modern American myth. The statistics are sobering; half the marriages in America "fail." Many young Americans have resolved not to marry, or have at the least concluded that serial monogamy is the preferred mode amongst heterosexual couples. Perhaps we need to reframe our old view of "failure" and admit that the old relationship paradigm does not always fit the accelerated demands on modern American adults.

Commitment is still the cornerstore of a healthy relationship. We must give ourselves over to another for the long haul, with the best of intentions. But relationships can and do run their course, complete their purpose, not always as "till death do us part" marriages. "What about the children?" you might ask. Children of single-parent family households are quickly becoming more the norm than the exception in our society. Our children are in the soup along with us; they often make better adaptations than adults. Marriage, after all, is for adults.

There is yet another ground of conflict, an inner struggle astir in each of us: we are each challenged to integrate an invisible partner, a male or female inner opposite within our own psyches. This synthesis of masculine and feminine is the psychological work that Jung considered the great opus, the masterpiece to which shadowwork is only the apprenticeship, the prelude. The inner marriage can be experienced as the dance of love, perhaps constellated through deep love for another. Or, it can be like a torturous crucifixion of longing, a struggle to find the creative union between masculine and feminine while living with conflict and difference in our outer relationships.

So, at least according to Jung, before we can begin the task of harmonizing the energies of male and female, within and without, we must first meet the shadow. It is paradoxical that this encounter can take place while in the presence of love. We think of the shadow as demonic and ugly, not a thing of beauty and truth. But love can be a gift from the gods—bringing us both profound bliss and profound torture—to trick us into wholeness. There is a higher calling in love, one that burns hot and pure and melts the oppositions within our breast.

Relationship provides us with the best mirror for self-knowledge. Neither the public arena nor introspection work as well, because intimate relationship acts like a crucible, a durable container for meeting the shadow. Through soul connection with another we become vulnerable, open to our own truths, more capable of withdrawing our projections and taking responsibility for those disowned parts. This can also happen in a therapeutic relationship; Freud thought of psychoanalysis as "a cure through love." But, romantic love is the ideal vessel.

We are all driven toward relationships, and yet our souls need autonomy. These are inevitably at crossed purposes, creating the most vexing of circumstances to endure in intimacy. When we are in love, we want to merge in union with the opposite-in-the-other, surrender to the powerful longing for connection, and even as we pursue this longing we fear we will be sacrificing our unique individuality to the other. But the shadow of love is more than fear, more than possessiveness or jealousy. We must also learn to accept what we cannot tolerate in the other and in ourselves.

In love, we also project the golden shadow, the nobler aspects that we fear in ourselves. It seems easier to burden another with our best than to rise to our true calling. Unfortunately, this way of loving—either in-love or hero-worshipping—deprives us of our own best possibilities. "Ignoring the gold can be as damaging as ignoring the dark side of the psyche," says the writer and teacher Robert Johnson:

> Curiously, people resist the noble aspects of their shadow more strenuously than they hide their dark sides. To draw the skeletons out of the closet is relatively easy, but to own the gold in the shadow is terrifying. It is more disrupting to find that you have a profound nobility of character than to find out you are a bum. Of course you are both . . . some people may suffer a severe shock or illness before they learn how to let the gold out.[2]

Falling in love is a divine madness, where we experience the beloved as a god or a goddess, shimmering with the numinous glow of archetypal potential. We are intoxicated with a kind of madness, an unrelatedness that ignores the unfinished human being before us. There is sacred power in love, but it also has this dark aspect: if we do not respect it, if we indulge ourselves and stay too long in the ecstatic or the euphoric illusion, we lose it. We must move from the archetypal energies that attract us and discover a more personal intimacy. The ultimate expression of our connection, as the Romantic poet William Blake suggested, is in creativity. We can keep the gift of love moving by bringing a full expression of the beauty in our relationships into the world.

In the following essay, "Gender Wars," by Aaron Kipnis and Elizabeth Herron, we meet 14 American men and women engaged in the contemporary dialogue between the sexes. We join the authors at a week-long "gender reconciliation council," conducted in a mountain wilderness area of Northern California. Seven women and seven men are present, many of whom are involved with the women's and men's movements. The women are camped at one edge of a glacial lake and the men are at the opposite end. Some of the time has been spent in same-sex "lodges." There have also been a series of group meetings with the other sex, encounters concerning both the differences and the shared challenges for members of separate gender cultures. We enter their dialogue at the beginning of the fifth day of the retreat.

—J. A.

Gender Wars

Facing the Masculine and Feminine Shadow

AARON KIPNIS
& ELIZABETH HERRON

I WOKE UP EARLY THE NEXT MORNING, just as the sun was emerging over the ridge. It was very quiet and peaceful. All I could hear were the sounds of a few jays squawking and the occasional plop of fish jumping in the lake. There was already a plume of smoke rising from the men's camp. I imagined, with some envy, that they were cooking trout for breakfast.

In the past, I've always relished eating the fish Aaron would catch. But now I wondered, why did he have all the fishing gear? And how come I've never bothered to learn how to fish myself? I guess it's because I don't like to get my hands all slimy with fish guts and so I just let Aaron do it all. But now, with him on the other side of the lake, I was resenting my lack of hunting power.

Last time we camped, I ran through the meadow and gathered live grasshoppers with Aaron. He said, "If you want to eat fish, you've got to help catch bait." Yech! But I got over my bug aversion. Clearly, I could also bait my own hook, catch, and ugh, even clean my own fish now. I was tempted to walk over to the men's camp and demand a fishing pole and tackle from them, but just about then Doris sat up sleepily in her sleeping bag and gave me a big grin.

"What a day!" she exclaimed, looking out at the mists swirling on the lake.

"Yeah, and what a night!" I answered, referring to last night's council.

We laughed together. One by one, the women got up and gathered around the fire. After four days in the wilderness, we were a motley crew. Yet, despite the lack of makeup, styled hair, and clean clothes, everyone looked more relaxed and vital than when we began our trip. When I'm out in the woods with Aaron, I often continue to wear a little bit of makeup, even though Aaron *always* quits shaving. But since I'd been in the women's camp, I hadn't bothered with my cosmetic mask, and neither had anyone else. The other women actually looked more beautiful to me now than they did the first day.

Each woman had courageously shared very intimate parts of herself over the preceding days. It made me feel a special closeness with them that transcended the brief time we had spent together. I felt as if these women had been sisters for years. While Lisa stirred a large pot of hot cereal, we started hashing out our feelings about our last meeting with the men. One of the observations that surfaced, after some discussion, was that although we obviously feared men's violence, we also resented men for denying their real vulnerability. The hero thing really turns us off.

Now, all of a sudden, we were confronted by a group of men who were admitting that underneath all the bluster, they weren't so tough after all. They were angry, hurt, afraid, lost, and troubled about a number of issues. Hey, they were human! They had feelings, just like us! At times, however, due to our conditioning to regard only stoic warriors who never complain as "real" men, we felt resistance to hearing men "whine."

Would "sensitive" men be able to protect us in a time of danger? Perhaps not. That was a troubling thought. As we talked about the council, however, we realized that we felt less angry with them because they had stopped bullshitting us and started telling the truth. And maybe, if we really wanted men to change, it was time for women to begin counting on themselves for protection rather than expecting men to keep on being the "tough guys."

The Victim and the Princess

"WHEN I HEARD THE MEN SPEAK with such honesty and sincerity, I was able to hear them in a whole different light," said Gloria. "It somehow helps me feel less angry to know that they also suffer. Honestly, before last night, I've never heard a group of men admit it. I guess that in the past I've really believed that men had all the advantages. Now I'm beginning to see another side to the story."

"I'm glad to hear Joel share his fears with other people," said Lisa. "It's no secret to me when the guy is in pain. The whole family is aware of it, even when he won't admit it. He'll come home after a stressful day and get mad at me or at the kids. But when I ask him how he feels he usually just says he's fine."

"Aaron says that *FINE* is a secret male code," I offered. "He calls it an acronym for *F*ucked-up, *I*nsecure, *N*ervous, and *E*xhausted." We all laughed.

"That's great," said Marie. "It sounds to me like a more accurate appraisal of the way most men really feel."

"It's sad that it's so hard for men to talk about their pain," said Doris. "Talking to other women about my problems keeps me going through the hard times. I couldn't do without it. Who do men reveal themselves to as they really are? How do they survive without brothers that they can confide in?"

"They don't survive," said Lisa, "that's the problem. That's probably why men drop dead eight years earlier than us. They can't ever show their real feelings. They get so bottled up that they just explode with heart attacks."

Women have always shared with each other both the challenges and pleasures of being mothers, lovers, wives, and workers. This process is an integral part of female culture. We've found a lot of self-empowerment *both* by getting mad about the inequalities we face and by revealing our wounds to one another.

But most men keep acting as if they don't feel much pain. So of course it's easy for us to assume that life must be much better for them. They've been keeping up the old John Wayne pretense that they can take a bullet in the chest and still just keep on riding hard, killing bad guys, and saving little ladies in distress. It makes us feel weak and stupid when we appear to be the only ones struggling. We began to realize that men, due to their conditioning to act like heroes, have been lying to us all along.

But they're not alone. We've also been lying. When we feign helplessness, it angers men just as much as their pumped-up posturing angers us. Men lie about their real vulnerability. But they are quick to reveal, and even exaggerate, their wealth and power to each other in the hope of being accepted and admired in male society. We women are in the habit of denying our real power, to one another and to men as well. But we are quick to share, and even exaggerate, our disadvantages and vulnerabilities, in the hopes of gaining sympathy and sisterhood.

I grew up watching old movies like *Gone with the Wind* and Errol Flynn's swashbucklers. I listened to powerful women like Aretha Franklin sing sadly codependent songs like "Rescue Me" on the radio. Wherever I turned, the same Cinderella messages were coming at me: "My Boyfriend's Back" (he's gonna save my reputation). None of the gender fables around me said, "Someday, Liz, you will be a powerful and successful woman in your own right."

Most women of my generation were raised to believe that some day the right man would come along and make our lives meaningful. The White Knight, we hoped, would rescue us from the dragon of our own emptiness, loneliness, and unrealized dreams. Although, many of us now consider ourselves beyond this old expectation, as I talk intimately with powerful women around the country, it's surprising how deeply ingrained this idea still is in our collective psyche.

We know that waiting for the perfect lover, perfect father, and perfect provider/protector to rescue us is a no-win situation. But this expectation persists. It's one of the biggest sources of our anger and resentment toward men—because no man can actually live up to this ideal. At least not for long. It's inevitable that we will be disappointed if we hold men to this standard.

One of the major archetypal gender themes of our epoch has been that of the Hero rescuing the Maiden from the Dragon. This story has deep resonances in all our psyches. It is the psychic matrix of our old gender culture. In this ubiquitous myth, the rescuer is almost always male. The victim in peril is female. In most of these stories, now represented by modern romance literature, the dragon is synonymous with a male victimizer whom the hero must defeat on behalf of the woman. This theme sells millions of books to women every year. One of the historical goals of the women's movement, however, has been the reimagining of this myth.

Over one hundred years ago Susan B. Anthony said, "Women must not depend upon the protection of a man, but must be taught to protect herself."[3] And in the century prior to that, in *A Vindication of the Rights of Women,* Mary Wollstonecraft said, "I do not wish them [women] to have power over men, but over themselves."[4] As these foremothers advised, women in quest of empowerment and liberation must examine their old, habitual identification with the role of victim and move beyond it. Thus far, however, despite its rhetoric of empowerment, the women's movement, *to the extent that it still perpetrates the cult of the victim*, has failed us.

Identifying ourselves as victims of the patriarchy has clearly been an important step in women's recovery and empowerment. It is part of waking from our slumber: the "feminine mystique" as Betty Friedan called it over thirty years ago in her landmark book by the same title.[5] There is a downside, however, to all our railing at men. In our anger at men for having some kinds of power that we lack, we frequently imagine ourselves as powerless. The devaluation of men, so rampant in today's feminist ideology, is often an attempt to make us feel bigger by making them feel smaller, rather than simply focusing on becoming more powerful ourselves.

When we believe that men have all the power and cause all the problems, then we believe things will only change when men change. At the core of this mind-set is the same dynamic that creates codependency in relationships. "If only he would change, our relationship would get better." This thinking leaves us at the effect of male behavior. We believe our world can only improve when he improves. If all power is seen as being outside ourselves, *then we feel no responsibility to change ourselves*, only to change the one with the power. The protected and "special" status of the "woman as victim" role puts all the locus of healing outside ourselves. The victim carries all the wounding and helplessness, the victimizer carries all the power and responsibility.

This is familiar ground for many women. It is part of our traditional upbringing to view the world in this way. Even many "new women" of the nineties, who have had their social and political consciousness raised, habitually fall into the same patterns. In many cases, they've been finding their sense of community through a shared sense of victimization rather than through developing a deeper knowledge and joy about their feminine power and magic.

Blaming men for "not doing it right" renders us helpless and passive princesses. Camille Paglia, feminist author of *Sexual Persona* says, "It is women's personal responsibility to be aware of the dangers of the world. But these young feminists today are deluded. These girls say, 'Well, I should be able to get drunk at a fraternity party and go upstairs to a guy's room without anything happening.' And I say, 'Oh, really? And when you drive your car to New York City, do you leave your keys on the hood?'"[6]

The Princess/Victim has no responsibility. And that's the great shadow allure of this archetype. Through embracing it we seem to magically become absolved of all our sins—"it's all his fault," we sincerely believe. Any attempt to point to our collusion in our own abuse or disempowerment is now called "blaming the victim." But the victim has no power! This sort of thinking has left women in some very abusive relationships. It has also, historically, left us out of the rough-and-tumble core of political and economic processes.

In the past, we primarily tried to influence policy through complaint. We were reactive rather than proactive. Now, however, more women are beginning to view themselves as equally powerful with men. We are competing directly with men for political and economic power. We are promoting the platforms we seek with a powerful proactive stance rather than merely reacting to men's ideas with resentment and protest. And we are realizing that being a warrior in the world of competition and power means that we will also, inevitably, get wounded.

The Princess, however, has a dense shadow. She genuinely believes that she should never have to suffer and that in a "just" society others should protect her from the hardships of the world. Just as the masculine shadow is often expressed in its actions, the feminine shadow is often reflected by inactions that have just as severe consequences for the world.

The recent changes in the gender mix of elected government officials is testament to the power of women who risk positively stating what they want and go after it instead of just blaming men for not relinquishing power to them. And we still have a long way to go. Therefore it is in the best interests of women, as we come into gender dialogues with men, to look carefully at our habitual identification with victimization and to stay aware of the disempowered consequences that this can bring us.

Women's arenas of power are often different from men's. There's no doubt that men in this culture have had more political and economic power than women. But women have incredible power to both create and sustain the relationships that weave the fabric of our culture. We have tremendous social, emotional, and intuitive powers. We have enormous sexual power that we've often used in shadowy ways throughout time to manipulate our world and achieve our desired goals. We have a different kind of power than men, which as many capable women have demonstrated, does not limit us or deny us access to men's traditional domains, but simply establishes us as intrinsically powerful beings in our own right.

The shadow of female identification with being helpless fuels and colludes with the shadow of the traditional male who is conditioned to be a hero—tough, capable, fearless, and "on top of it." It's a bad dream that men and women dreamed together. Now we're attempting to wake up. This is not an easy task. And it is especially difficult for any one side of an equation to change, in a vacuum, without the other.

In her book *The Ravaged Bridegroom,* Marion Woodman writes about the unconscious feminine and the unconscious masculine that get in the way of men and women claiming a new vision of partnership. She says, "The old petrifying mother is like a giant lizard lounging in the depths of the unconscious. She wants nothing to change. Her consort, the rigid authoritarian father, passes the laws that maintain her inertia. Together they rule with an iron fist in a velvet glove. Mother becomes Mother Church, Mother Welfare State, Mother University, the beloved Alma Mater, defended by Father who becomes Father Hierarchy, Father Law, Father Status Quo."[7]

The Hero

WE WENT OUT FISHING AT DAWN. The freshness of the morning uplifted my spirits. I watched the mists swirling over the lake and fondly imagined that Liz was enjoying the same fairyland spectacle from her side of the lake. Everything was perfect in our silent world until Dave suddenly cried, "Shit!" He'd taken a cast that somehow wound up with the hook in his thumb instead of a trout. It was stuck in deep. The only thing to do was to push the hook through so that the barb came out the other side. I cut it off with the wire cutters on my leather-maker knife and then backed the shaft of the hook out of the wound. It left two holes in his thumb.

A lot of blood spurted out and it was clearly very painful when I pushed the hook through. But Dave never winced or cried out. When I asked him if it hurt he replied, "Nah! It's just a little prick." I thought about the countless times in my life I had heard a man or a boy deny his pain. "Big boys don't cry," just about every man is instructed along the way.

Just as many women in the past found solidarity and membership by identifying themselves as victims, men have also found brotherhood and community with other men by joining the cult of the Hero. All our cultural directives—from early education and parenting, through adolescent sports, military induction, and initiation into the workplace—inform a man that in order to be well regarded by others, he must learn to model himself after a heroic ideal of masculinity.

In ancient mythology, this ideal was developed through heroic dramas about bigger than life characters like Heracles. Most of us learned about him as children in fables that extolled the virtues of his great strength that he harnessed to overcome seemingly impossible tasks. The name Heracles means "Glory of Hera."[8] In the Greek language, Hero means a man who is sacrificed to Hera.

The myth of Heracles has pre-Christian roots. He was called the "Prince of Peace, Sun of Righteousness and Light of the World." Like Christ, he descended into Hell and battled the Lord of the Underworld. And like Christ, he returned to the world above and was given a second birth and immortality.[9] These pre-Christian myths, like the story of Christ himself, have been major influences on the way in which we idealize masculinity as embodying the archetype of the Savior/Rescuer/Knight/Hero.

Ancient mythology gives us a glimpse into the collective psyche of a particular culture and epoch. One thing myth tells us is how that culture imagined gender. In the same manner, even though contemporary literature and other arts serve a similar function, cinema and television are the primary arenas today in which the archetypal forces moving though our collective consciousness are displayed. The heroic archetype that Heracles once represented is still very lively in the collective imagination of the American male.

Today, the archetype of the near invincible hero is carried in the roles played by actors like Arnold Schwarzenegger, Steven Seagal, Sylvester Stallone, Jean-Claude Van Damme, Dolph Lundgren, and Bruce Willis. In the past, it was men like John Wayne, Clint Eastwood, and Charles Bronson. These few men, and others like them, account for hundreds of millions of dollars in box office receipts every year.

Regardless of whether the role is Rambo, Rocky, Terminator, a Cliff Hanger, or a Super Hard-Ass Kung-Fu Cop, the theme, in most of these contemporary films, is remarkably similar. Just like Heracles, the male hero defeats a seemingly superior opponent against impossible odds. Often he is up against an extraordinary number of very vicious, powerful, heavily armed men. Yet, he has absolutely no fear in the face of superior forces. And he is never confused about the best course of action to initiate.

The hero inevitably suffers a great deal of physical abuse. He endures hardships that seem far beyond the endurance of any mortal man. Yet he, like Dave, expresses no complaint in response to his wounds, nor to his apparently hopeless situation or his exhaustion. In most cases, along the way, he rescues a woman in distress. Most often, he uses superhuman strength and fighting ability to defeat all the bad guys.

In some cases, there is variation on this theme. In the 1980s and '90s we began to develop a new modern, "soft" hero who is less heavily armored. He is represented by characters such as Daniel Day-Lewis' Last Mohican, Harrison Ford's Indiana Jones, and Richard Dean Anderson's MacGyver. Instead of brute strength and ultra-violence, these more politically correct heroes, in almost every case, use uncanny stamina, superior reflexes, and brilliant ingenuity to rescue the woman.

What's wrong with being heroes? Essentially nothing. Every one of us must connect with our own personal heroics in order to write a book, raise a child, start a business, face an illness, or engage in any of the hundreds of human endeavors that require us to overcome our fears of transformation, failure, injury, or death. The problem, for many men, however, is that they feel that they must *always* be heroes.

Even a completely rehabilitated chauvinist, as depicted by Bill Murray in *Groundhog Day*, must also face his own death several times, perform a variety of charitable acts, save a little boy's life, learn to play classical piano, and learn everything about the personal likes and dislikes of the woman he is pursuing. He must perform at a level of accomplishment way beyond the capacity of most mortals in order to be loved by a woman who doesn't have to do anything but look cute in order to win this sort of heroic attention from him. For many men, cinema imitates life to the extent that it articulates the unreal, heroic ideals that they feel they are expected to live up to.

The Hero and the Princess, like the Victim and Victimizer, are a split archetype. They are aspects of a wholeness separated into its parts. Each one of us has a courageous hero and a sensitive child within our psyche. Each of us has a ruthless streak and a portion of ourselves that feels wounded by others' ruthlessness. Problems arise when any one of these psychological elements dominates our character. We become "possessed" by the split-off part that, in acting out its polarized role, is also constantly seeking its missing part.

Heroes seek dragons to slay and maidens to rescue while princesses languish and pine for their princes to come. But both these positions are weak. After decades of women's books, the perils of princesshood are now painfully clear to most women. With only a few years of reflective thought about masculinity in our culture thus far, however, the deadly trap of the hero is not as obvious to most men.

In many ancient tales, the hero is sacrificed to the goddess. The martyrdom of Christ embodies this idea that the ultimate goodness of a man is expressed in his willingness to die for others. This belief led countless generations of men to heedlessly march off to slaughter in wars. My generation of men was called cowardly for suggesting to the world that the time for peace had come; not through more fighting to end war, but by ceasing fighting altogether. The Knight needs armor to fight when there is clearly no other recourse. But, as I discussed in my last book, *Knights Without Armor*, when he forgets how to remove it, he becomes trapped within his strength and is unable to tend the wounds that lie hidden beneath his hard exterior.[10]

Another shadow of the Hero is his incapacity to forge meaningful connections with others. Just as hysteria was the dominant psychopathology attributed to women in the nine-teenth century, narcissism has become the primary psycholog-ical dis-ease of contemporary men. The cinematic hero, like so many males these days, is excessively narcissistic—solitary and self-involved. These prominent icons of heroic masculinity believe that they, and they alone, can solve the problem of the day. They have contempt for conventional rules. They often solve their problems, one of which is often rescuing the girl, by direct, compelling ultra-violence.

Of course we need heroes in times of distress. And it's com-mendable that women and men, in times of great danger, do reach beyond the ordinary limits of their bodies and emotions. As Liz articulated earlier, the problem for women occurs when they habitually act like victims. And, similarly, the problem for men emerges when they become habitually heroic.

Heroes can't ask for help when they need it. Men caught in the heroic archetype often suffer greatly and die early deaths. They've been trained to believe that they don't need anyone but themselves. This is the dark side of the heroic archetype. Just as over-identification with the Victim/Princess cuts women off from their power, over-identification with the Hero cuts men off from their feelings and their capacity to provide sustained care for themselves and others.

The heroic ego is cut off from the myriad denizens of psy-che which have the capacity to enrich the lives of men. The inevitable consequence of heroic identity formation is that of psychological impoverishment. The void that grows within the inner shadow of the outer-directed hero is intimately linked with the self-abuse many men inflict on themselves. This abuse often takes the form of alcohol and drug abuse, workaholism, domination of women, and other obsessions that enable men to stay in heroic denial about their pain, their emptiness, and their human needs for connection.

The Dark Goddesses

"IN LAST NIGHT'S COUNCIL, I was surprised to hear about how afraid the men are of women," said Susan, leaning against a tree as she caught her breath. We had decided to take a hike up a trail to a smaller lake. It looked nearby on the topo map, but we had yet to find it and had stopped for a break on an outcropping of rock that offered a panoramic view of the Grace Lake valley.

"Me too," agreed Marie. "I was floored. I've always thought of women as the 'gentler sex,' but to hear the men talk, you'd think we were going to murder them while they slept."

"More likely bewitch them and steal their power," laughed Doris, as she used her bandanna to wipe the sweat off her face.

I reminded them that men's fear of women is nothing new. World mythology is replete with images concerning the destructive aspect of the feminine. In India for example there is Kali: a goddess of death with a necklace of skulls, wielding knives and scissors, fanged, drooling, and wrathful who sits astride the corpse of her husband, Shiva, in necrophiliac conjugality. Her images are absolutely terrifying.

"I've always thought of the feminine as being compassionate and merciful," challenged Lisa. "The Goddess as I understand her is the embodiment of the good mother."

"That's certainly one aspect of the Goddess," I replied. "But there are also many nasty and violent goddesses. In this country people have primarily worshipped the Virgin Mary, who's very pure and good—an image that many women have felt they must live up to. And the more recent resurgence of interest in women's spirituality has also emphasized the all-nurturing symbol of the Earth goddess. But that's only a piece of the story."

Our Judeo-Christian culture is very dichotomized in its thinking about good and evil. Unlike many native cultures, which hold a paradoxical view of their gods as combining equal portions of good and evil, we tend to split the archetype and locate all light or darkness in one or the other. This philosophical fracture in our thinking also fuels the tendency of both genders to locate all the goodness in one sex and all the evil in the other.

A fundamental principle of archetypal psychology is that there's a danger of becoming possessed by that which we fail to commune with. The degree to which any group denies their own shadow is inevitably equal to the need they have to project the blame for all their sorrows on others. If we fail to attend to our shadow, we breed denial about our own capacity for abuse. Denial about the potential for abuse of power is dangerous in any group. At this stage in our council, we're trying to move forward by looking at some of the shadow issues that we drag along as women. One aspect is clearly our addiction to identifying ourselves as victims. The other is our denial of both our real power as women and our capacity for violence that, in many cases, matches that of men.

Men, due to their greater strength, do significantly more damage in domestic assaults, but many studies indicate that women initiate and instigate just as much domestic violence as men. They actually strike the first blow in a majority of domestic disputes.[11] It is culturally sanctioned for women to slap men when they're angry; we see it in films every day. Women also perpetrate the majority of physical abuse and battery of children, particularly male children. The incidence of child battery of both sexes is over twice that of sex abuse, the abuse category dominated by males.[12] Current studies indicate that females also commit about one-third of the sexual abuse of underage males, another fact which is usually unreported when women berate men for their abusiveness.[13]

The essential nature of women, as well as men, is a complex mixture of qualities. It does us a disservice to deny our capacity for violence because then we also inevitably deny our power as well. There are huge historical and mythological fallacies inherent in idealizing the feminine principle as only benign and life-engendering. The dark Goddess is a ubiquitous, integral part of the feminine principle.

In Greek mythology, from which many of the images and ideas for our own culture grew, there are harpies and shrews, the Gorgon-Medusa who turned men to stone, Scylla of the whirlpool, dismembering maenads, furies, and sirens—all seducing men into their deaths. The crone Hecate, who on one hand has a rich store of ancient wisdom, is simultaneously dry, cold, and withering. Demeter, a goddess of generativity—the harvest goddess—also has a wrathful form in which she threatens to destroy all human life unless her daughter is released from the underworld. Artemis is a beautiful nature goddess who loves wild animals, but also wields arrows and transformative spells, and destroys men for simply sighting her in the woods.

Golden Aphrodite also has her dark side. She's a wrathful destructress and a jealous, manipulative dominator of her son, Eros. She reflects the same dark face of the matriarchy as expressed by Psyche's vain and jealous sisters who, in the story of Psyche and Amor, oppose her marriage with Eros, calling him a monster when in actuality he is divine and beautiful.

The Egyptian goddesses Ta-urt, Nekhbet, Am-mit, and Amam are also terrifying devourers, as well as the Aztec goddess Coatlicue and the Mayan Ixchel who caused disastrous floods.[14] The Germanic goddess of the Underworld, Hel, is from whom arose the name for the Christian purgatory—Hell.

The Navahos have Snapping Vagina who is malevolent, violent, raging, and destructive. She's eternally hungry, embodying a vast emptiness. She kills by engulfing her victim.[15] Also in Navaho myth, which springs from a matriarchal society, is a power-driven, plotting sorceress named Changing Bear Maiden, who kills her brothers after turning into a monstrous bear. She is also called Maiden-Whose-Clothes-Rattle. She wears sharp deer hooves that cut and hurt men, and then she possesses them.[16] In her book, *Changing Woman and Her Sisters*, Sheila Moon surmises that this aspect of the goddess has "a marked and negative ambivalence towards that which is living."[17]

There exist hundreds of other personifications of the Terrible Mother from almost every culture, throughout the millennia. These images—like the ravaging mother protecting her young in the film *Alien*—are no mere apple-eating Eves, invented, as many feminist writers would have us believe, by a gynophobic (woman-fearing), patriarchal culture. They express an essential archetypal element present in human consciousness and nature itself—the wild, primitive aspect of feminine sexuality and the all-devouring aspect of the Earth. When women embrace the role of the innocent victim, all their power, willfulness, and rage gets stuffed into the shadow. When we relegate the Dark Goddess's heat to the closet, it starts to smolder. Before you know it, what might have been a small flare turns into Mt. Vesuvius.

So I suggested to the women, as we got up to continue on our hike, that we open up the door of the closet and see what might be lurking there. I reminded them that, before our next council, we still had the task of exploring what gets in the way of our creating genuine partnerships with men.

"What kinds of things do *we* do that are abusive to men? What are our feminine styles of dominating and deceiving?" I asked. "Are there ways we attempt to cope with our victimization by evoking the dark mother? How does our suppressed power come out? Do we cut them to shreds verbally like the Navaho goddess with her sharp hooves? Do we dominate and possess men by swallowing them like Snapping Vagina?"

We walked in silence for a bit, doing some heavy thinking. The trail rounded a bend, and there was the long-awaited lake. Within minutes we had stripped off our clothes and jumped in. Later, as we dried off in the sun, Doris picked up the thread of this topic and spoke up.

Witches, Bitches, and Whores

"OKAY, I'LL BEGIN. I have an nineteen-year-old son. His father ran off with another woman years ago, when Danny was small. I was terribly hurt and as Danny grew up, I continually bad-mouthed his father. I feel bad about it now, because it ruined their relationship. My ex-husband tried to keep in touch over the years. He clearly wanted to be part of Danny's life. But I wouldn't let him. It's been very hard on Danny not to have a father, and I could have made it possible if I hadn't been so angry. His father really isn't such a bad guy, he just didn't love me anymore. I never forgave him for that."

Marie then spoke about her ex-husband. "I was married, before Larry, to a man who put me through law school. He got me started in my career and then our marriage fell apart. I used all my new legal skills and my feminist 'take no prisoners' approach to men and money, to take him to the cleaners financially. He ended up paying me alimony for years before I remarried, even though I was making more money than him.

"If I had been treated like a man in the divorce, I'd be paying him or putting him through school until he could make as much as me. Now I have a great career but he's stuck with a contracting business that's going bankrupt. And he's getting too old to be a carpenter again, the only other trade he knows. When I was listening to the guys talking the other night, I started thinking about Daniel, and how I really should make some kind of amends to him."

"Well, I find this difficult to tell you all," Lisa began, looking down at the ground. "Even though in my women's studies classes I'm a champion of women's and children's rights, something I've never disclosed is that I've abused my own kid. There was a period in the early years of our marriage when we were very stressed out. We were struggling financially. Joel was working two jobs, one of them at night. I was also working at a lousy job during the day. I'd come home at night exhausted, and Gabe was often fussy. Sometimes I would just start screaming at him. A few times I lost it altogether and just started smacking my son around. It was as if I was possessed by one of those furies you mentioned, Liz."

"It's easy for me to imagine how that could have happened," said Merle. "I've been very close to hitting my kids at times. But my shadow is that I had an affair behind Alan's back. It was pretty sleazy and didn't last long, but it still almost destroyed my marriage. When he found out about it, instead of taking responsibility for getting sort of swept away by this hunk at the health club, I blamed Alan for not being a good lover. I really made him feel like shit."

"I've done some pretty outrageous sexual things too," said Susan. "I seduced my boss last year and ended up with a promotion that beat out several other qualified men. That's probably the real reason that there's so much hostility towards me at the office. I think they've guessed. I've also sexually used men purely for my own gratification without any intention of forming a relationship with them. I've been pretty ruthless when it comes to my sexuality. By the time I was thirteen years old, I learned that I had power over men. I like using it, but clearly have a double standard about men who behave the same way."

Gloria was next. "I guess what I need to get out of the closet is the raving bitch that I am with Jerry sometimes. I am good with words. I can tear him to shreds. The poor guy doesn't even know what hit him. When I'm angry, I shame him without mercy. He doesn't even defend himself anymore, which seems to make me even angrier. I'm ashamed to say that there's a part of me that feels strong knowing I have this power over him."

After a few minutes without anyone else speaking I said, "I seduced a sixteen-year-old boy when I was about thirty. I was married to my ex-husband then, and he had this cute young guy working for him on his crew. I became totally possessed and just couldn't keep my hands off this kid. He thought it was great to have sex with an older woman. But if it had been reversed, if I had been an older man with a younger girl, it would have been considered statutory rape or child molestation.

"I don't know if it screwed him up or not, but since I've been with Aaron, and heard about how many men in his groups have psychological problems and sexual dysfunctions related to early seductions by older women, I've begun to wonder about this. Was I an educator/initiator, as I've always imagined, or just a selfish user? I'll never know. But it's clearly in our shadow as women that we carry such double standards about sexual encounters with underage girls or boys."

One of the most glaring fallacies of the modern myth of the ideal feminine and the evil masculine is the tremendous denial of the capacity inherent within women for the abuse of their own feminine power. Psychologist Herb Goldberg sums it up by saying that, "for every chauvinist who uses women, there is a woman who uses wiles, coyness, helplessness, and other 'feminine' manipulations to gain her end and goad him into proving himself the big man, the succeeder, the dominant, fearless, powerful protector."[18] If we are ever to have peace with men, it seems we must begin openly acknowledging our part in creating the conflicts between us.

The Male Monster

THE MORNING'S FISHING HAD BEEN FRUITFUL, despite Dave's wounding. And this time I went out with Jerry and Dave, while others stayed behind tending camp. That felt good. As I returned to camp, I was thinking about the topic for the next council. What do we do as men that gets in the way of partnership with women? What is our part in the war between the sexes? I noticed that I was having a lot of resistance to this step in the process. It was easy to talk about our anger in the previous talks, somewhat more difficult to talk about our fears and our grief, but it now felt significantly harder to consider taking responsibility for things being the way they are.

Over the years, as I've worked with thousands of men, a primary issue that keeps presenting itself is men's struggle to recover from a deep, personal, and collective sense of shame. This feeling is not easily articulated by men. More often than not, it's denied until we have done some trust-building and created a safe environment in which men feel they can reveal their truth without becoming further shamed.

Shame makes its presence known by the destructive behaviors that men engage in as an attempt to either repress or escape from the debilitating depressions associated with unhealed shame. These actions, as we discussed in our look at the diseases of the hero, often take the form of excessive drinking, drug abuse, workaholism, addiction to high risk excitement, sexual obsessions and even acts of violence against others who are perceived to be the inculcators of that shame.

In ever-increasing numbers, teenage boys are shooting one another on the streets of our nation for "dissing." In 1992, over 800 young men were killed in the Los Angeles area alone, more than in the war zones of Beirut, Palestine, or Northern Ireland.[19] The slang word "dis" comes from disrespect. The street code says: "If you try to shame me, or my friends or family, I just might kill you." This is one of the most extreme examples of male incapacity to bear shame.

In the cases of many of these youths, their shame has grown over a lifetime of emotional impoverishment and a severe lack of economic and educational opportunity. Often their violence appears to be way out of proportion to the acts that provoke it. It only appears "senseless," however, when one overlooks the many social injustices men face such as single sex draft registration, twenty times as many deaths on the job as women, and significantly higher rates of incarceration, homelessness, and victimization by violence.[20]

Men are biologically programmed to be more aggressive than women, but they are not destined to be more violent.

There have been many cultures in which men were not significantly violent. Violence does not come out of a vacuum. Often a man's violence seems senseless until we examine the broader context of the social context that shaped his character and either directed his aggression into creative acts or fueled his rage and pushed him toward destruction.

Low self-esteem is a life threatening disease. When it gets bad enough, men commit suicide, four times as many young men as women. Or, in many cases, when someone, inadvertently or otherwise, exacerbates that low esteem, a man will strike out. This dynamic is often present in men's abuse of women. When all our feelings of inferiority are denied and relegated to the shadow, it is assured that a posture of superiority will develop in the personality as compensation. A great deal of feminist writing depicts violence towards women as part of a vast and conscious male conspiracy to keep women from having power. What seems more true, however, if one analyzes case histories, is that, in many cases, men become abusive of women because they are afraid of women's power to shame them by casting a spotlight on the inferiority hidden in their shadow.

Shame is immobilizing. Guilt makes you feel that what you did is wrong. You can survive it and learn from it. Shame, however, makes you feel that *who* you are is wrong, and many men will go to violent extremes to avoid that deadly feeling. Consequently men are often reticent about consciously revealing their shadows. They often feel that to do so will only put another nail into their coffin of immobilizing shame.

One of the many wild beasts associated with Dionysos was the goat, who was also sacred to many Earth-based deities like Summerian Enki as well as Greek Pan and Hermes who, like

Dionysos, were very sexually oriented, "earthy" gods.[21] Sylvia Perera notes that Azazel was the early Semitic goat-god from whom our term "scapegoat" arises.[22] Every year, on Yom Kippur, a live goat was driven out of the camp deep into the wilderness, with the sins of all the villagers ritually heaped upon its back.[23] The scapegoat carries the split-off shadow of any particular group. For centuries, Judeo-Christianity projected its shadow onto women and women's sexuality. Currently, many men feel that their gender and sexuality have become the new scapegoat for all the wounded feelings in our culture.

In light of all this, a good portion of my work in the past has centered on helping men to recover from the scapegoating that shame projected on them. In my protective and nurturing role as a leader of men's groups, I have tended to resist the "monsterization" of masculinity so prevalent in ideological feminism and have focused instead on supporting and helping to actualize the inherent goodness in all men.

Now, however, as I returned to camp and ate breakfast trout while discussing the council of the previous night, it seemed that the time had come for us to look fearlessly at the ways in which men are, in fact, monsters. If there is ever to be peace between the sexes men must begin to acknowledge their real responsibility for destructive past behaviors and make amends wherever possible. Women do have good cause to fear us. Not only because men are capable of destroying nature, and dominating, raping, beating, torturing, and killing women, but because—all sociological analysis aside—there is something deep within the male psyche that is cold, dark, and utterly unfeeling that allows men to behave in this manner. Mythology is replete with these images of the dark masculine—the Monster.

Contemporary culture is fascinated with the male monster. The bulk of our horror films are concerned not with the Dark Mother that men so fear, but rather with the hidden and dark, monstrous male that sexually exploits, stalks, terrorizes, wounds, rapes, or kills women. Over two hundred films have been made on the theme of the Vampire alone. Although there are female vampires, they are usually servants of the primary male monster or mortal women whom he has subverted to his will. Vampirism is imagined as a masculine force that preys upon the life's blood of women, particularly young and attractive women. The Werewolf is also most often male, as are most other Creeps, Beasts, Things, and Its.

Another related genre in film and literature is that of the human monster—the psychopathic killer. From *Scarface* to *Silence of the Lambs*, in well over 90 percent of thrillers, the human monster is male. Freddy Kruger of the *Nightmare on Elm Street* series and Jason of the *Friday the Thirteenth* series take this genre to macabre new heights, adding an otherworldly dimension to their psychopathic powers.

What are these films telling us about the male psyche? What was fueling the fear the women at Grace Lake had so openly shared with us? Scapegoating and the projecting of our own shadow on the other gender is clearly one aspect of the enmity between the sexes. But another aspect is the apprehension of the genuine destructive powers of the other sex. Just as the dark feminine has the power to smother, dominate, poison, seduce, and sexually manipulate men, the dark masculine has equally strong powers to dismember and destroy the lives of women.

Most horror stories, about which literally thousands of films have been produced, have common themes:

1. The monster is male.

2. He is ruthless (*Cape Fear*), obsessively focused on his prey, relentless, and devoid of compassion.

3. He preys on women (*Psycho*), usually very young, sexually alluring women (when he kills men it's usually incidental, because they somehow got in his way).

4. He is either utterly devoid of feeling or takes a certain sadistic glee in his slaughter (*Nightmare on Elm Street*).

5. He is usually immune to tactics that would kill ordinary men and often repeatedly rises from the dead (*Terminator 2*).

6. He is cold-blooded, dead-eyed, and often has hypnotic powers over his prey (*Dracula*). In short he has many reptilian qualities. Descriptions of a man who exploits women include a "snake," a "worm," or a "slime."

The Monster lives hidden in the shadow of the Hero, and as such he shares many of the characteristics of the Hero. Many of our contemporary tragedies emerge from the shadow of heroic activity. The destruction of the environment and over-population are shadowy by-products of heroic good intentions. The Monster is strong, purposeful, fearless, and practically invincible in battle. He is a relentless and dauntless stalker. If we probe more deeply into the ancient structure of the male psyche, we find at its foundation a Hunter. For millions of years the primary occupation of men was hunting. It's what we're built for.

Men's greater stamina, muscular strength, skill at stealth and stalking, capacity for one-pointed focus, and stoic response to pain and discomfort are all required skills for successful hunting. These are also the attributes a man needs to be a skilled warrior. So when these abilities are used in the service of others, and especially where they are protecting and supporting women, then we call the man a Hero. When these skills and powers are used to stalk and prey on women, however, then the man becomes a Monster.

Much of our modern language regarding the sexual pursuit of women is in the language of the hunt. Men go out "cruising" (stalking) to get "a piece of ass" (game, meat) and say they "scored" or "got laid" (were successful hunters). Unless he misses, a man only hunts an animal once. Once he has scored, the animal is dead. After satiation and rest he hunts again.

Agriculture brought about animal husbandry, and men developed ongoing relationships with animals. Romantic bonds with women also seem to have evolved more deeply during this time. But there is still something deep in the male psyche that is only interested in the hunt and not at all interested in developing a relationship or intimacy with his prey, except as some sort of lure to capture them with. This is the mode of sexual predators such as the young men who gained notoriety for their participation in the "Spur Posse" sex-point scoring gang in California. This is the sort of behavior that infuriates women. Women feel betrayed when men use the promise of intimacy as a lure for sex, and it breeds the deepest of resentments against men.

The Monster seems connected with the older brain in men, something neurophysiology calls the "reptilian brain," what Freud, from a psychological perspective, called the Id, or what many religions, from a spiritual point of view, refer to as the demon within. There is an aspect of male sexuality that is purely reptilian, predatory, and narcissistic. This is the thing that women fear. The Hero is in the business of rescuing women from their fears. That's why in mythology, as with St. George and dozens of fairy tales, the Hero is depicted slaying a reptile, the Dragon. Although classical Jungian psychology imagines the Dragon as a negative mother complex, it is archetypally a much more complex image. In contemporary cinema, the hero slays not the old earth mother but rather the reptilian bad guy, the "cold-blooded" killer.

On one hand, conscious men are trying to escape the bonds and burdens of living up to the Hero archetype. It's oppressive for a man to feel that he always has to be strong, can never show fear, and can never ask for help. But on the other hand, there is an aspect of the Hero, what we might call the *sacred* Warrior or Hunter, that is sorely needed in this time. There is real evil in the world. Our cinema monsters hardly do justice to the real monsters of our last century: Hitler, Stalin, Ceavsescu, Pol Pot, and the Serbians who practice "ethnic cleansing" through the systematic rape of tens of thousands of women.

The horrors of this world, the starvation of entire populations, the destruction of complete species and whole ecosystems, the degradation of the ozone shield above our heads, are all man-made. And we need real heroic Warriors, both male and female, to meet these Monsters and defeat them. A first step toward becoming a sacred Warrior must be to confront the monsters within. If we have not done so, how can we ever act in a trustworthy manner in the world? That seemed to be the task that faced us men before we met with the women again. The Monster is representative of when man's best capacities to defend, nurture, and to create life, are turned in the direction of destroying life. Darth Vader (the Dark Father) was a noble Jedi Knight, before he was seduced by the dark side.

The Monster and the Hero are another split archetype. All the exploitive power is in one and all the nurturing power is in the other. The Monster, Hero, and Victim are all part of the same psychic complex. In most stories, it is the male Hero who defeats the male Monster in the service of the female Victim/Princess. Instead of defeat, however, what is needed is awareness of and reconnection with our split-off parts. Because, as our horror tales tell us, the monster is never really defeated. He just vanishes for a while only to rise again in the sequel.

Were the women at Grace Lake right to fear us? Are we so evolved as to be free from the sorts of behaviors women fear? Or have we, in resistance to our shame, denied the ways in which we are also monsters alongside our noble capacities to nurture and defend? And so, I asked, for the first time in a gathering of men, "Who amongst us has raped or battered women or simply had fantasies of hurting, dominating, or sexually exploiting women?"

Bastards, Batterers, and Fiends

DAVE WAS THE FIRST TO SPEAK. "When I was in the seventh grade we used to have folk dancing after school once a week. There was this one girl, Nancy, who would usually wear a pleated skirt. When we twirled around, her dress would come up and I could see her pink panties underneath. Those panties, and the shape of her buttocks standing out against them, had the most disturbing effect on me. For months afterward I would masturbate with the fantasy of touching her naked bottom. I don't know why she affected me that way, but I used to sit in class behind her and frequently think about those pink panties coming down around her knees.

"I don't remember ever having a sexual fantasy before then. Certainly I never saw any dirty pictures and no one ever told me about sex. I just started out my sexual life obsessively. I don't know why. Now it's Susan's ass that's in my mind. A part of me is more into women's asses than their personalities and I know that is degrading to women. I feel like if I ever shared this story with women, they'd regard me as some sort of deviant. But I really don't know how to not think about it. It's like not thinking about an elephant when someone mentions one."

"The head of my department is a woman," said Joel. "She's very demanding, critical, and humorless. Some of the students refer to her as the 'High Priestess of Political Correctness.' I've begun to have fantasies of raping her. It's weird, I guess. I really love Lisa and I don't usually have many sexual thoughts about other women. But with this woman, my fantasies are about getting even somehow for all the humiliation I, and others, have suffered around her.

"Another way I deal with her is by trying to make her feel stupid and incapable even though she's a brilliant scholar. I'm always vigilant for the *slightest* inconsistency in her ideas. I feel that if I was more of a warrior, as you say, Aaron, I'd confront her more directly about her behavior without attempting to shame her in public meetings or dominate her in my fantasies. But the way I deal with it is by thinking about tieing her up in her office and bending her over her desk and . . . well, you get the picture."

"I battered Merle once," said Alan. "It's a family secret I've never told anyone about. It was early in our marriage. I had just lost a major contract, was scared about my business failing and was drinking too much. She started giving me a hard time about something or other, I don't even remember what. But I slapped her pretty hard. And then when she started screaming at me, I slapped her a few more times.

"She ran out of the house with a split lip and drove off to her mother's house. She didn't come back for over a week, after many phone calls and assurances from me that it would never happen again. And it hasn't, even though there have been other times when I felt like it. It scares me. My mom used to scream at me all the time. I often wished I could have hit her and made her stop. Maybe I was getting back at Mom. I don't know, but in any case I don't ever want that to happen again. I still feel bad about it, especially when we visit her mother, who's never returned to the level of friendliness she had toward me in the past."

I confessed that when I was 14 I slapped around my girl-friend for going out with another guy. In the culture I grew up in, that was what was expected. But then the next day her big brother showed up and punched me in the nose a few times. He told me that if I ever hit her again he'd kill me. I never hit another woman after that. As I told this story it made me think that as part of our accountability to women about our own vio-lence that it was also necessary for us as men to commit to con-fronting and preventing the violence of other men. We can do this through education, mentorship, and where appropriate, as in the case of Linda's brother, a serious display of strength.

Andy told us a story about a time when he was a freshman in college. After a night of partying with a date he invited her back to his room. They started making out and when the girl asked him to stop, he didn't. He said "By the time she said no, she was half undressed and I was completely aroused. And so I just kept persisting until she finally gave up and had sex with me. Now I understand it was date rape. Even though I think of myself as a gentle man, who is generally respectful of women, it's also true that I have the capacity to rape."

Larry told us that he had had a sexual affair with a close friend of Marie's. "Even though I didn't beat or rape anyone I feel that this is a violent thing to have done. I betrayed my marriage vows. And by doing it with a friend of Marie's, I feel like it was a double betrayal. The affair lasted about six months, during which time I had very little sexual interest in Marie. That just added to the hurt."

Jerry was the last to speak. He was silent for a while as we looked toward him expectantly. "Soooo, Jerry," said Dave eventually. "What about you?"

"Well, I just don't have any violent thoughts about women and I don't have any weird sexual needs either," he said somewhat defensively. "I'm glad to hear the rest of you admitting that you have problems with women. But I love women. I haven't ever wanted to hurt them."

"Bullshit," said Andy, "I just don't believe you. Come on, Jerry, 'fess up, what's your deep, dark secret? If you leave here without saying it, I think you'll never be free. You'll always be feeling guilty around Gloria. Look, I've seen the two of you together and I know something is going on in that relationship that you're ashamed about. I can see it in your body language. You're the one that's always challenging the rest of us to come clean about our attitudes towards women. I don't think you're being straight with us now."

Jerry just sat there, glowering at Andy and avoiding eye contact with the rest of us. After a while he took a deep breath, looked up at us and said, "Okay. You're right. I'm copping out here, doing the very thing I have accused most of you of over the last four days. I'm going to tell you something that I've never told anyone.

"I have a sister who is two years younger than me. One summer when I was about sixteen we hung out a lot together. We had a lot of fun taking hikes and going to the beach. She's was pretty mature, physically and emotionally. She was already having sex with boys and into other stuff, and I began to notice that she was starting to look terrific in a bathing suit. Anyway, one night Leslie and I were home alone for the evening. I got stoned and she was in our parents' hot tub. She invited me to join her. I did, and after a while I put my arm around her. We were just sitting there. It felt very innocent. We had always been close. Anyway, I had my eyes closed and she leaned over and kissed me, very sweetly and tenderly.

"Instead of pushing her away I just sort of kissed her back. She was so pretty and it just felt so good. I kissed her some more and then I fondled her breasts. I felt full of love for her and got very turned on. I kissed her breasts and one thing led to another, until we had sex. I knew we shouldn't, but I just couldn't find any restraint. During the next few months we had sex a number of times until she got a steady boyfriend and demanded that we stop.

"We never told anyone about it, and we've never talked about it. But she's in therapy now, twenty years later, and I recently got a letter from her requesting that I help pay her bill. I'm painfully aware of the fact that she must be dealing with her issues about the incest. I guess that's one of the reasons I've been so involved in all this women's work with Gloria and even facilitated groups for abuse victims and offenders. I've been living a lie all these years. It's a relief to finally admit the truth to someone."

Andy put his arm around Jerry and comforted him. Here we were, good fathers, committed husbands, environmentalists, psychotherapists, educators. We were men who, for the most part, were consciously concerned with the betterment of humankind. And yet, it was undeniably clear that within every one of us lay the seeds for violence and the abuse of women. What we could do to assure that those seeds did not find fertile soil in our souls and those of other men was one of the tasks that lay ahead of us.

Both our groups had taken a look at some of the secrets locked away in the dark and dusty rooms of our psyches. The next step in our council was to find a way to reveal the paradoxical truth of our existence to one another. We had to find a way to help one another come to terms with the fact that we were all capable of violence toward the other gender while simultaneously wanting to learn how to more deeply love and nurture the other.

PART IV

Sexuality

Introduction

A lot of things wrong with society today are directly
attributable to the fact that the people who make the
laws are sexually maladjusted. "Why should those
dirty teenagers have all the fun?"

—Frank Zappa

Anyone unable to understand a god sees it as a devil.

—Joseph Campbell

HONORING THE PLEASURE PRINCIPLE is a confusing
subject in American life. We have so many sources of
gratification available to us, greater than at any other time in
human history, and yet, when we are honest with ourselves, we
must admit to an underlying sense of guilt about sensual pleasure. We carry a disturbed relationship to pleasure, a split
between sexuality and relationship, that has been reinforced by
hundreds of years of subtle and not so subtle societal taboos,
sanctions that have been transmitted through the generations.
What we may actually feel about love, sex, and pleasure is often
confused with the messages we each have received, directly or
through osmosis, from our parents and elders.

This repression of sexuality—sexuality in the broad sense,
the totality of pleasure in human relationships, from caring

and affection to tenderness and touch and the act of sexual intercourse itself—is easily misunderstood because of our outward permissiveness. Though many Americans enjoy a high standard of living, all the creature comforts and then some, our materialistic indulgence is filled with contradictions that produce both pride and guilt. In some quarters, we are even the target of ridicule. One no longer has to be a Communist to criticize the materialistic fallacy in our culture. It is an open secret: We have plenty of seductive titillation with little orgasmic release.

If we look at the underbelly, we see that Americans aren't really happy with this way of life. There is widespread violence, depression, and anxiety in our country, much of it the by-product of sexual repression, oppression, and confusion. The antidotes aren't much better: more prisons for the antisocial elements, and pharmaceuticals such as Prozac and Valium for the weary. The signs of our discontentment are everywhere. Just listen to what the artists of propaganda are telling us from Madison Avenue. Notice how easily their symptomatic message preys on our sense of incompleteness and displeasure, how tempting it is to believe in the simplistic solutions they offer. "Have a soft drink for the short-term fix," or, "eat the right snack to get yourself up." For the long-term pleasures you'll need to drive the right automobile, you'll want a svelt, unblemished, and undernourished body that smells antiseptic and sweet. Make sure you obtain the correct products at the right stores, the specialized appliances, the latest fashions, and the politically correct foods, furnishings, and widgets. And if you want the cybernetic buzz, you might go for the high ticket items at your local electronics emporium, stereos and computers that can razzle-dazzle you and keep you transfixed, even when you run out of surplus cash.

When people speak of Americans as sexually repressed, it produces dissonance. Such analysis doesn't fit our popular view of ourselves: What repression? As a nation, we seem hell-bent on pleasure. In fact, many believe our society is too permissive, that we are a self-indulgent, hedonistic nation of conformists, that we live in a purgatory of earthly delights with no true pleasure, morality, or ultimate values, and no hope of redemption. However, peel away the mask and we see that this external view of permissiveness is really based on a denial of pleasure and sensuality. We seem to have substituted products and activities that can "safely satisfy" us, that have the look and feel of sex, but which actually sublimate our longing for human relatedness and sexual fulfillment, and which dodge any challenge by the prevailing prudish attitudes.

We may have explicit sex on TV, and pornography on newsstands and in rock lyrics, for heaven sakes, but for many it is difficult to show affection in public without feeling embarrassed and ashamed. Pornography, carrying as it does our repressed sensuality, surfaces as a shadow symptom. If we can set aside the prurient interest and the dominance genre of pornography, this explicit material shows us a positive, guilt-free reminder: We all have instinctual, aggressive sexual feelings in our bodies, positive life energies that can be owned without retribution. Physical sexual expression is natural and essential, even in times of overpopulation and AIDS. Of course, there is a wholesome side to sexuality; it works best in a container of mutuality and love. And it requires creativity and productivity in the other spheres of our lives, in order to balance the compulsive nature of sexual urges.

What is most repressed in America is the body. We can use it for work or athletics, or for looking good, but the physical body as a source of pleasure is still a forbidden fruit. The body lies almost hidden in the shadows in our Judeo-Christian culture. In spite of sexual revolutions and a whole literature dedicated to reclaiming Eros, the erotic has remained demonized for millenia. Our collective mores portray sex as sinful, and whether you subscribe to them or not, they force upon us a split between sex and human relatedness. No one in our culture is immune from this damning influence. It is a struggle to humanize our sexual lives, to balance the tension between containing *and* expressing our powerful sexual feelings. We have been hypnotized to believe that performance and control determine sexual pleasure. We are unsure whether it is safe to trust the natural intelligence of our bodies. We hesitate, fearing we might lose rational control, as if we might degenerate and, as John Lennon humorously suggested, "do it in the road." When it comes to actual sexual contact with another, we are still rebellious adolescents, stealing our pleasure in the backseat of a car.

We can trace our modern struggle with the sexual shadow to the 19th century manners of the Victorian era. Sigmund Freud's early work in psychoanalysis established the first real advances in bringing sexuality out of the shadow. With this important work by European psychologists—Freud's on sexuality and Jung's on the shadow—we have gained considerable ground in releasing sex from the confines of an archaic morality:

> Because of the time and circumstances in which he lived (middle-class Vienna at the end of the nineteenth century), Freud believed that the repressed evil that men and women feared was entirely sexual. His systematic investigation of this aspect of the Shadow, combined with the coincidental decline in the power of the Judeo-Christian super-ego, did much to purge our culture of its erotic demons, enabling many previously repressed compo-

nents of the Shadow to be integrated within the whole personality of individual men and women without forcing them to suffer the concommitant guilt which would certainly have afflicted earlier generations. This affords an impressive example on a collective scale of the therapeutic value attributed by Jung to the analytical process of recognizing and integrating components of the Shadow.[1]

In the following essay, Dr. Robert Stein, a European-trained American analyst, continues in this tradition. He has dedicated his life's work to the recovery of our instinctual life by healing the splits between body and soul, sexuality and love. In his essay, "Sexuality, Shadow, and the Holy Bible," he adds a heretofore missing dimension to our view of sexuality: there is a god in the dis-ease, he reports, a sacred force of great power in our natures that has been suppressed by our theologies. Focusing on the rituals of psychotherapy and contemporary coupling, Stein resurrects this primeval force in our understanding, pointing the way to once again connect passion and heart with our sexuality. This is a vision that offers hope for opening the true potential of our sexual lives, detailing a way to reclaim the energy and power hidden in the darkest corners of the American shadow.

—J. A.

Sexuality, Shadow, and the Holy Bible

ROBERT M. STEIN

OUR PURITANICAL PATRIARCHAL HERITAGE has cast a heavy shadow on sexuality and the body. This projection of the shadow onto sexuality has had a profound effect on the American psyche. My use of the term shadow is in the Jungian sense; on the personal level it refers to all those parts of ourselves which we experience as unacceptable or repugnant to cultural standards or to idealized images of ourselves, and which we tend to project onto others; on the collective level, the shadow is the personification of Evil.

The Holy Bible tells us that before the Fall the human animal was pure and innocent and free of sin. Satan in his serpent form changed all that when he enticed Eve to eat the forbidden fruit. According to the myth, our ancestors lost their innocence as soon as they became aware of their nature and ashamed of their sexuality. Our Christian culture, with the help of such saints and philosophers as Augustine and Descartes, has cultivated this polarization between spirit and nature, saint and sinner, good and evil. *For Christianity, sexuality is the shadow.*

Depth psychology has shown us that the more we reject the shadow the more power it gains over us. Psychologically, something is basically wrong about turning our backs on Satan. Could our culture's obsessive fascination with all things sexual be a manifestation of how the disowned shadow operates?

Could the current epidemic of sexual abuse to children and women be another manifestation? I think so. How can we individually and as a culture change our basically hostile attitude toward our sexual shadow?

Sexuality is a great power. The ancient Greeks had gods such as Pan, Hermes, Priapus, Dionysus, Aphrodite, who personified various aspects of this power. In contrast to our monotheistic Judeo-Christian tradition, paganism honors all the gods. Jung's archetypal perspective has made us aware that the soul is essentially pagan and that many aspects of the soul suffer from neglect when we worship only one god. I see the fundamental hostility of our Christian culture toward the body and the passions of the flesh as largely responsible for our culture's disastrous relationship to basic human needs.

I remember a vision I had as I sat with a colleague in a restaurant overlooking the Santa Monica Mountains in Los Angeles in January 1960. I had recently returned from Europe where I had been in Jungian training and on a deep inner journey for almost four years. The vision:

A council of Native Americans were meeting in the mountains. They were enraged at the destructiveness which the white man had inflicted upon their sacred land. They were predicting our destruction if we continued to dishonor their earth Gods.

This was at the beginning of a decade in which the youth of our nation initiated a great revolution which threatened to overturn the powerful puritanical work and anti-sexual ethics of our American culture.

I began my therapeutic practice wearing mostly dark suits, white shirts, and conservative ties, very conscious of my need to maintain my medical persona. By the end of the decade, I had hardly a suit or tie in my wardrobe, and *I had become much more concerned about being human than about being professional.*

Well, all that has changed drastically in recent years. Most of my colleagues are now terrified of transgressing professional boundaries. And suits and ties have long been back in style.

Since the care of the soul has fallen into the hands of psychotherapists in this century, it may be enlightening to see how the Puritan and Christian fundamentalist projections of the archetypal shadow (Evil) onto sexuality is affecting this honorable profession.

About four years ago my malpractice insurance carrier sent out an astonishing notice announcing, without any explanation, that they would no longer defend any physician who was accused of having had undue intimacy with a patient. Obviously, they were referring to erotic intimacy, but the statement reflects the generalized fear of any type of intimacy in the therapeutic relationship. Even in traditional western medicine, the physician–patient relationship involves intimacy as well as objectivity. But to expect psychotherapists to practice from some fantasized position of scientific objectivity and distance is utter madness. I wrote a long letter to the board of directors of the insurance company explaining my viewpoint, and I also suggested that by taking such a position they were inviting even more lawsuits. To my amazement, within a few weeks I got a letter from them telling me they had dropped this new exemption. I relate this incident only as an example of the current hysteria surrounding our fear of sexuality. I will return later to other examples.

The hysteria which has been building up around the legitimate concern about sexual transgressions has many aspects to it that resemble the "witch hunts" of our Puritan ancestors. However, as Jungian analyst and author Adolf Guggenbühl-Craig has suggested, instead of wanton, voluptuous women being accused as the evil agents of Satan, men are now the accused.[2]

With the demise of communism and the withdrawal of the projection of Evil onto Russia, sexuality has once again been reinstated as the Devil. Our politicians, who for decades have been able to use the image of the Evil Russian Empire to divert our attention from the truly dehumanizing shadows of our own political system, have all too eagerly joined the anti-sexual bandwagon. Unfortunately, at the forefront of this modern witch hunt are many feminists, who must surely be unconscious of how much they are embracing our western patriarchal view of sexuality and the body. The anti-abortion movement is another anti-sex-for-pleasure movement with many characteristics of a "witch hunt." Even the tragedy of AIDS is being used to reinforce our puritanical attitudes toward sexuality. *Puritanism has always been more comfortable dealing with the evils of sexuality than with the evils of patriarchal oppression to the human spirit.*

While Puritanism denigrates the sexual deities by rejection, persecution, and repression, the type of promiscuity that accompanied the sexual freedom movement of the '60s is also a de-sacralization of sexuality. The current AIDS epidemic has certainly forced the homosexual community to reexamine their attitudes toward sexuality. Perhaps this tragic affliction will eventually lead our whole culture to reexamine our relationship to the sexual gods and to establish a more favorable relationship to them.

Phallos and Psychoanalysis

PSYCHOANALYSIS BEGAN WITH FREUD'S DISCOVERY of the unconscious sexual origins of hysteria and neurosis. Freud's biologic orientation prevented him from realizing that rejected and dishonored pagan phallic gods were being revealed in our neurotic symptoms. Jung, in transcending scientific materialism, was able to contribute a deeper dimension to our understanding of neurosis.

Even though Jung disagreed with Freud's insistence on the exclusive sexual origins of neurosis, his investigations led him to the insight that many neurotic symptoms and complexes can be seen as a manifestation of the return of the pagan gods which our Judeo-Christian culture rejected.

Powerful phallic gods are involved in all sexual transgressions. Since the penetrating, fertilizing power of Phallos is essential for change, I believe we need to give high priority to establishing a more favorable relationship to these rejected pagan deities. Pan, the god of all nature, personifies this divine generative life force. He is the goat-god: hot and hairy, phallic, roaming, goatish. "As the human loses personal connection with personified nature, and personified instinct," says archetypal psychologist James Hillman, "the image of Pan and the image of the Devil merge. Pan lives in the repressed which returns, in the psychopathologies of instinct which assert themselves (according to Roscher) in the nightmares and its associated erotic, demonic, and panic qualities."[3] As long as we continue to reject Pan, the sexual instinct will always be experienced as potentially dangerous to the morals of our culture.

Hillman develops the idea that the image of Pan chasing the Nymph contains both the compulsive desire and the terror evoked by the sudden eruption of the sexual instinct.[4] Contained in this archetypal polarity of attraction and repulsion, desire and inhibition, is the key to understanding the process through which instinctual compulsion can be modified through imagination.

The Incest Wound

THE CAPACITY TO CONTAIN THE TENSION of the opposites is essential to human psychological development. The incest taboo, which is universal, functions mainly to gradually develop this capacity in the child. In my book, *Incest and Human Love*,[5] I proposed that both the incest desire and the taboo are instinctual qualities typical of the human condition, and that the tension between the desire and inhibition promotes psychological development.

The Polynesian verb *tapui*, from which the word "tabu" originates, means "to make holy," "to set apart." The incest taboo, by sanctifying or deifying the parental couple, creates a psychological distance which is essential for the development of consciousness. In this way, an aura of mystery begins to surround the parents, stimulating the child's imagination to focus on the special qualities of mother and father and their relationship. This unique human veneration of the parents stimulates the release of the archetype of the Sacred Marriage (the alchemists' *hieros gamos*) and of the child's first experience of its human incarnation. This image, which Jung has called the Incest Archetype, expresses the harmonious union and polarity between the masculine-feminine opposites, a root metaphor for the union of all opposites. Jung describes this archetype as an image of the supreme union of the opposites, expressed as a combination of things which are related but of unlike nature.[6]

When a culture loses touch with the profound meaning of the incest mystery, the forms and rituals for transforming the incest libido deteriorate, and children will experience deep, splitting wounds to the soul. In my book I argue that psychologically the incest taboo functions positively as follows: 1) to stimulate the sexual imagination and the formation of the image of marriage as a Sacred Union, the *hieros gamos;* 2) to make us aware of our incompletion; 3) to stimulate our desire to attain completion, first through union with another but ultimately through an internal union. I also argue that *contained within the polarity of the incest archetype are both desire and inhibition, and that the tension between these opposites is essential to psychological development.* I propose that the repression of either the desire or inhibition causes splits in the child's psyche between love/sex, mind/body, spirit /flesh. I coined the term *incest wound* to describe these developmental splits.

For example, a very prevalent pattern is a father, who suffers from an incest wound, projecting his idealized image of the feminine onto his daughter; their connection becomes very strong and erotic. Because of our culture's loss of connection to rituals for containing and transforming incestuous imagery, neither father nor daughter can allow erotic feelings or imagery to enter consciousness. If this repression of sexual imagery and feelings is reasonably successful, there can be a number of consequences:

1. The child becomes unconscious and cut off from her naturally erotic nature. Since she can more easily block out sexual feelings and imagery than control the spontaneous reactions of her body, a split occurs between the upper heart and mind centers and the lower sexual centers of body consciousness.

2. Along with the fear and repression of sexuality, the child gradually begins to fear any natural spontaneous expressions of her nature because the "dirty secret" might pop out if she reveals her true self. In other words, the self gets buried along with the forbidden sexuality. With the emerging self blocked, the child develops an identification with a non-threatening self image, which is always false because vital parts of her nature are excluded.

3. Because father, too, must repress his sexuality, he is also fearful of the spontaneous expressions of the self, so he ends up playing the archetypal role of father rather than being himself.

4. With the projection of father's anima or soul-mate image onto the daughter, an unconscious spiritual marriage is formed which causes another split because the conscious and sexual marriage is with mother. Psychologically, the daughter then falls into the role of the "other woman," and she feels both guilty and superior to mother. On one level she wants to get rid of mother so that she can have father all to herself, but since on another level she needs mother's love, she is thrown into a love/hate ambivalence. But mother, too, is into a similar love/hate ambivalence because she experiences daughter as the other woman. When the split is severe, this often results in a deep mutual rejection.

Many women end up by totally rejecting mother or anything to do with motherhood, and they remain identified with the daughter archetype for the rest of their lives. Because of the repression of the natural self and the fear of revealing it, no one involved in an incestuous triangle is able to be truly himself or herself.

Out of her guilt, the daughter may fall into the role of the good and obedient child, or she may feel so betrayed and rejected by mother that she becomes the angry, rebellious child. When her sexuality begins to blossom in puberty, the split becomes even more severe and the relationship to father becomes increasingly fragmented. Often, the desperate need to break away from home is linked to a rejection of such family dynamics and a need to get free of the oppressive soul-splitting incestuous triangle. Instead of experiencing the attraction and harmony between the masculine/feminine opposites, the child experience these archetypes—sun/moon, yang/yin, heaven/ earth, spirit/flesh—as hostile opponents. In psychotherapy, I believe the desperate need to heal this split is often at the core of the so-called transference neurosis.

Depending on the severity of the incest wound, a child may be forced to repress all sexual imagery in order to be sure that none of the guilt-provoking fantasies invade his psyche. Fortunately most children do not have to use such extreme measures, but when they do, it results in an overwhelming fear of sexuality and a severe blockage of the sexual instinct. Such children have a tendency to panic at the slightest sign of losing control. More typically, children are able to allow non-incestuous sexuality to enter consciousness, but the incest wound still prevents feelings of kinship connection and all the romantic, loving fantasies of spiritual intimacy from entering the psyche along with the sexual imagery. Thus, the incest wound is directly responsible for this common type of internal split between love and sex, between the spiritual and sensual portions of the soul. When the tension between the incest desire and prohibition is obliterated, fragmentation results and the essential internal union between the masculine/feminine opposites is not possible.

I believe the severity of the wound can be measured by the degree of fear one has of losing rational control, even if that fear is not directly related to sexuality. Why is there such horror of losing rational control, of allowing irrational, spontaneous emotions and desires to express themselves without ego censor? Is it because we fear going crazy, behaving shamefully, animalistically? What is going on inside when we are caught in this ego trap that makes us so mistrustful of our instincts? I recall a shocking dream I had when I first became aware of the depths of my own incest wound: I go to my office for something. It is late at night, about 11:00 P.M. As I open the door I suddenly become frightened, sensing some ominous presence in the room. I switch on the light, but see no one. Suddenly, I hear a noise like a whimper coming from behind me. I turn to discover a small, ragged twelve-year-old boy crouching under my desk. I awakened terrified. Later, using the technique of active imagination which Jung suggests, I reentered the dream in fantasy: I pull the frightened boy out from under my desk and demand to know what he is doing there. At first he refuses to answer, but finally he tells me that he hides under my desk all the time when I see patients. Then turning to me with a lustful grin, he says, "I really dig all those sexy stories your patients tell you." I become furious, call him a sex maniac, and threaten to turn him over to the police. Then he breaks down sobbing and my heart goes out to him. Between sobs he tells me how I had abandoned him when I was twelve because of my own sexual guilt and that I forced him to go underground out of fear of my own lust.

Obviously this little boy was an image of that part of me that I had repressed. One can imagine how fearful I must have been at the time of this dream of losing rational control if all my repressed incestuous sexuality lurked just under the protective front of the physician's desk.

Such examples of the soul-splitting effects of repressed incestuous sexuality are plentiful and relatively easy to grasp once they have been revealed. However, many other expressions of the incest wound are not so obvious. For example, sexual desire may not become fully aroused except in a triangular situation. As soon as the triangle is broken the desire often disappears or diminishes. This may seem contradictory because one would expect that the incest fear would inhibit sexuality in a triangular situation. However, we must not forget that the purpose of the incest taboo is to prevent a child from having sexual union in those relationships where he feels the greatest spiritual intimacy. Thus incest guilt can be avoided as long as one is unaware of experiencing one of the opposites, love or sex. The repressed opposite will, however, continually threaten to reenter consciousness because of the soul's fundamental need for union. In other words, *the longing for incestuous union, even though it is repressed, is as powerful as is our horror of violating the taboo.* The more we repress the desire the more power it gains over us, so that we are continually fascinated by and falling into incestuous types of involvements. So long as we remain unconscious of the repressed other half, we do not experience the guilt and painful conflict. Innocently we plunge from one relationship to another, emerging each time fragmented and disillusioned.

Another very common manifestation of the incest wound is the experience of loving someone sexually and spiritually in fantasy, but of being cut off or unable to express such feelings in actuality. This situation often occurs because of the fear of consciously embracing the phallic or aggressive aspect of the sexual instinct. The incestuous guilt associated with aggressive sexuality prevents such people from initiating the flow of Eros, although they may be very responsive to the initiating action of others. In this way they can remain unconscious of their own aggressive impulses and continue to feel innocent. I recall the sexual fantasy of an extremely passive, but sexually promiscuous woman, whom I saw some years ago. In order to masturbate to orgasm, for example, she needed to fantasize that she was in jail and being forced to masturbate by the jailer. Only with this type of fantasy could she let herself surrender to her sexuality without guilt.

The desire for incestuous union will be activated in every relationship which offers the possibility of soul connection. If this desire remains unconscious, it has the effect of obstructing

the natural, spontaneous flow of love because the incest archetype always demands eternal commitment in a sacred marriage. Simply put, if I feel compelled to make a permanent
commitment every time love moves me toward union with
another, will this not make me cautious and fearful of loving?
One must be free to love or not to love, free to feel and express
love in the quick of the moment whether or not it lasts forever.
The incest wound interferes with this freedom because of the
soul's longing for the sacred, eternal union with its mate. This
longing for eternal union needs to be experienced as a psychic
reality or it will continually interfere with our capacity for intimacy by demanding literal fulfillment whenever one feels love
for another.

Apart from love and sex, the incest wound tends to interfere with the experience and spontaneous expression of all the
aggressive instincts. For example, a son will fear standing up to
his father and revealing his own aggressive potency because of
his guilt about his unconscious incestuous marriage to mother.
In the language of Freud's Oedipus complex, the guilt toward
father coupled with the fear of castration eventually becomes a
part of the internalized parental authority or superego. The
more severe the wound, the more the child experiences the
inner parent as rejecting of his nature, especially of his aggressive sexual nature.

Let us not forget that the incest wound refers to the split
which occurs in a child's psyche usually as a result of the
repression of sexuality in relation to a parental figure. When a
parent projects the soul-mate ideal (anima or animus) onto a
child, guilt, fear, and repression of sexuality usually occur in
both of them. As a consequence, the incest archetype splits
and the soul is fragmented. This obstructs the natural, spontaneous, soulful experience of intimacy between parent and

child. The child will then feel the same incestuous guilt, fear, and splitting in any experience where parental love and erotic feelings of intimacy occur simultaneously. Since the sense of stability, structure, and permanency in any relationship is a function of the parental archetypes, the incest wound tends to cripple the sexual instinct as soon as a relationship begins to feel stable and permanent.

The sacrament of marriage binds the couple to each other and gives them communal recognition as a social unit committed to mothering and fathering a family of their own. Resistance to marriage is often a fear of falling under the power of the parental archetypes where love becomes a passionless duty and sex becomes a dirty, loveless, masturbatory act. Of course, I am describing the traditional puritanical split which Freud first observed. Our late twentieth century sexual mores have considerably altered this picture (at least before the AIDS epidemic) so that we are more able to be sexually open and sensually free nowadays without feeling sinful. But the incest wound still makes it difficult for us to open up to the union of love and sex, spirit and body, when the parental archetypes are constellated as they are in marriage. One of the reasons falling in love is such a wonderful experience is that we feel whole and healed and at one with the cosmos. Even the deepest incest wounds are temporarily healed. But as soon as Eros and Aphrodite move on, the old wounds begin to reappear.

Many couples are able to experience an intimate, vital sexual connection with each other, but their hearts are closed during the sexual act. Before and after intercourse, they may feel tender, caring, protective, and spiritually intimate, but it is as if they have to let go of those sentiments in order to get with their sexual passion. Other couples have great difficulty experiencing sexual passion with each other as soon as the love affair is over and the parental archetypes enter, which often occurs on the wedding day. When this happens sexuality may be totally blocked or it tends to be unconnected and masturbatory. This used to be a dominant pattern in our culture, but it seems to be shifting as a result of the cultural acceptance of the joys of sex.

Still, the roots of the incest wound run deep so that marriage relationships tend to become progressively less erotic as couples begin to carry more and more of the parental images for each other. Even in those marriages where the sexual passion is kept alive, I believe this seldom occurs unless the woman has a strong identification with the Love Goddess and is so cut off from the mother archetype that the mother image is only minimally constellated in the marriage relationship. Such women tend to have disdain for their own mothers and are very rejecting of the mother role for themselves. They also tend to fall heavily into a daughter role with their husbands and with most men. Because of the profound spirit/sex split, these women can often be very open sexually in spite of the heavy father-daughter relationship which is usually constellated with their husbands. This is so because the split enables them to be sexually open yet spiritually closed during sexual intimacy and thus not vulnerable to the negative, threatening aspects of the father archetype. Consequently their sexuality remains unconscious and therefore unable to enter into the humanizing light of spiritual love.

Since so much of our sexual aggression and passion is contained in our repressed incestuous desires, keeping sexuality alive in a legitimate relationship such as marriage is difficult because only forbidden, illicit erotic imagery can release the repressed instincts. Many couples keep the erotic tensions going by having illicit affairs or by creating jealousy-provoking situations that stimulate the sexual imagination. Some couples use pornographic material to release their sexuality and others can achieve orgasm only when they are able to lose themselves in very specific fantasies. I don't mean to imply that the fascination with images of forbidden sexuality is pathological, but only that the *dependency* on such images for the release of sexuality is a manifestation of the incest wound.

The depth of the incest wound is determined by the severity of the psychic split between love and sex, mind and body, desire and inhibition. In my view, *the wound to the soul from the repression of sexuality can be as damaging as actual sexual contact between parent and child.* The current myopic focus on the literal violation of the incest taboo is unfortunate because it has diverted attention away from deeper, more relevant psychological issues. Unfortunately, *nothing is more damaging to the child and to its rich imaginal life than literalism.*

An adult who suffers from a profound split between his or her rational, responsible, ego-controlled self and the vulnerable, imaginative, spontaneous childlike aspects of his or her being will become progressively narrow, rigid, and arid. The greater the internal split, the more desperate is the need to unite with those qualities of innocent wonder, openness, softness, and virginal freshness which the child carries. This sort of split is probably a major factor behind the compulsive need of many adults for sexual intimacy with children. The soul's need for union is often expressed in images of sexual intimacy. Healing does not lie in attempting to overcome these "perverse" desires, but in being able to experience fully the incestuous desires emotionally and imaginally. In this way the sexual drive is gradually transformed, and the child (inner and outer) can be loved, honored, and respected as a vital part of the soul and as a unique being.

The current hysteria about incest and sexual molestation intensifies the fear of sensuality and sexuality between parent and child instead of inspiring us to find a new, creative relationship to the incest mystery. I suggest that the primary function of the incest prohibition is to stimulate the imagination and to bring instincts into the service of love, kinship, and creativity. This means that the experience of an erotic flow and connection between parents and children without fear, guilt, or violation is essential to the psychological health and maturation of the child.

Pan and Psychotherapy

OUR FEAR OF SEXUALITY is fundamentally related to the mistrust and fear of the soul. The soul is much too irrational and unpredictable for the rational mind. Sexuality is a metaphor for all those spontaneous, irrational, unpredictable qualities of soul which are always a constant threat to the "well-ordered" life.

Pan's instrument is the body, and it is in our emotional-bodily centers of consciousness that we experience him. In the psychotherapeutic situation, the cultivation of such body awareness is a *sine qua non* to honoring this dishonored god. If our fear of Pan is displaced toward our fear of violating social mores and professional ethics, as I feel Peter Rutter has done in his recent book,[7] then we cut ourselves off from the compulsive Pan energy which can only be transformed by reflection. In describing his "near-sexual encounter with a woman patient (Mia)," the critical moment occurred when Mia slid gradually off her chair and sat cross-legged in front of him as she tearfully related a humiliating experience she had had with a man. As Mia edged her way toward him and began to bury her head in his lap, he says, "I was overcome by an intoxicating mixture of the timeless freedom, and the timeless danger, that men feel when a forbidden woman's sexuality becomes available to them."[8]

Resisting the intoxicating power of his sexual desire, Dr. Rutter asked Mia to return to her chair, which she did without hesitation. "In our respective seats," he says, "we were able to begin a therapeutic exploration of the way, in her blind search for a man's comforting warmth, she had offered herself repeatedly to men."[9]

Rutter views Mia's seductive behavior and his overwhelming desire to succumb to the allure of forbidden sex only in terms of his patient's self-destructive pattern of repeatedly offering herself sexually to men in power out of her desperate need for warmth and comfort. [10]

I don't question this perspective, but I suggest that when we shift our view of such transferential constellations to the Pan/Nymph archetype, the profound healing value of holding the tension between the desire and inhibition becomes meaningful. No one can fault Dr. Rutter's ethics in the way he handled his erotic intoxication. But one wonders if a deeper healing might have occurred if he had been able to hold the tension of the opposites and talk with his patient about the feelings both of them were experiencing.

Let me suggest that unless Pan can be experienced and honored in all his awesome numinosity, no healing of the fragmenting incestuous wounds to the soul is possible. *The reflective act of holding the tension between Pan's compulsive desire and the nymph's terror is essential to this process.* Not for a moment do I mean to suggest that this comes naturally or easily. Nevertheless, cultivating the capacity to contain the erotic energies released when the powerful Kundalini Serpent (the primordial erotic life force) is awakened is essential to both psychological and spiritual development. D. H. Lawrence expresses this same idea in another way:

> Mentally, we lag behind in our sexual thought, in a dimness, a lurking groveling fear which belongs to our raw, somewhat bestial ancestors. In this one respect, sexual and physical, we have left the mind unevolved. Now we have to catch up and make a balance between the consciousness of the body's sensations and experiences, and these sensations and experiences themselves. *Balance up the consciousness of the act, and the act itself. Get the two in harmony. It means having a proper reverence for sex, and a proper awe of the body's strange experience* . . . [my emphasis].[11]

Hillman further amplifies the image of Pan chasing nymphs as follows:

> Pan goes after nymphs, that is, rape aims at forms of indefinite consciousness located still in nature, but not personally embodied. . . . The nymph is still attached to woods, waters, caves, wispy figments, mistiness; she is chaste, nature still intact, a maiden. . . . Rape puts the body's drive toward soul into a concrete metaphor. It presses the soul into concreteness. It forcibly ends the division between behavior and fantasy, violating the soul's privileged distance to live life through reflection and fantasy. Pan the raper will be conjured up by those virginal aspects of consciousness that are not physically real, that are "out of touch," unsensed. Feelings and thoughts that remain wispy and flighty, that still are cool, remote, reflective will call rape upon them. They will be assaulted again and again by concretism.[12]

I have become increasingly aware of how frequently my analysands are in their heads and cut off from their bodies, and of how often the analytic work tends to become intellectualized when this happens. At such times Phallos often enters out of the desire to penetrate the intellectual barrier and make a connection. This phallic thrust may come as a spontaneous erotic feeling, impulse, or image, or it may express itself through my efforts to penetrate to the underlying meaning of a dream or behavior. Pan chasing the nymph is one way of gaining insight into such experiences and also their potential for violation. Lest we get stuck in literalizing the sexual imagery, let us remember that many more analysands are being raped daily by analysts' ideas and interpretations than by their sexuality. If the therapeutic relationship is to facilitate a healing of this split between Pan and the nymph, between body and mind, then reflection upon these images is essential.

Depth psychology has made a significant contribution toward healing the wounds to the soul by creating a ritual which provides a safe environment for cultivating soul and for exploring the nature of our difficulties in the areas of love, sex, intimacy, self-expression, and creativity. Contemporary psychoanalysts (including Jungians) continue to stress the therapeutic relationship as central to this endeavor. The analyst's character and his or her capacity to model a spontaneous, flexible, non-authoritative humanness seem to me to be essential to this healing process.

The current trend to literalize the archetypal parent–child aspects of the therapeutic relationship makes the therapist totally responsible for protecting the "innocent and powerless child" from any of the therapist's feelings which are not beneficial to the patient. This undermines the intimate nature of the therapeutic relationship. The fear of Eros, and the denigration of the phallic gods is behind this attempt to codify the psychotherapeutic relationship. Not only is psychological development and the transformation of Eros not possible in such an unsafe environment (the analyst must also feel safe), but the patient is infantilized and robbed of his or her power. A deep healing of childhood wounds to the soul is obstructed under these conditions, and the future of depth psychology is in jeopardy if we fail to address this issue and succumb to the panic about sexual transgressions.

Viewing sexual transgressions in the therapeutic relationship *only* in terms of the therapist's abuse of power and the psychological reenactment of incest is a reductive move which: 1) invalidates the experience of soul; 2) depotentiates and pathologizes the numinous healing potential of the powerful gods involved in such transgressions; 3) deepens the incest wound by perpetuating the soul-splitting love/sex, mind/body dichotomy and the analysand's view of being either the innocent victim or sinful, seductive child. This is not to question the importance of the power and dependency issues evoked by the archetypal parent-child constellation, but rather to emphasize the importance of the deep symmetry which occurs in therapy as soon as two people commit themselves to the care of the soul.

A dedicated, ethical therapist who concretizes his or her sexual desires in the therapeutic relationship must certainly be possessed by the Pan/Nymph archetype. How else can one explain a therapist risking the potential humiliation of professional condemnation, loss of livelihood, and hard-earned professional credentials? Ethical, moral, and legal approaches to the problem miss the point. I am arguing that such states of erotic possession stem from the repression, denigration, and fear of the pagan gods.

The Shadow of Objectivity

MY BOOK, *INCEST AND HUMAN LOVE*, which I subtitled, *The Betrayal of the Soul in Psychotherapy*, is a plea to reevaluate the soul-splitting Cartesian foundations of Western culture so that we can find better ways to heal our deep universal incestuous wounds. When the book was first published in 1973, it was radical, but now it is even more so. I worked on this book for about ten years, all through the revolutionary decade of the '60s. It was my way of coming to grips with the forces in our culture that were fragmenting to the soul. I felt psychotherapy perpetuated this dehumanizing splitting between mind and body, spirit and nature, by insisting that the therapist remain always objectively detached and personally unrevealing.

What we have done to the ecology of our Earth, to the world soul, is but a reflection of what we have done to our own souls. The current hysteria about maintaining boundaries, particularly erotic boundaries, so that therapy will be absolutely safe for the innocent, vulnerable, helpless "inner child," is sterilizing therapy and infantilizing patients. In our culture children have been psychologically damaged more frequently by parents who are trying to live up to some idealized image of a good parent and fearful of being themselves than by parents that have been sexually or physically abusive. The attempt to "clean up" therapy is intensifying the profound mind/body, spirit/nature split which our culture has condoned. Without a radical change in attitude and philosophy, therapy can only perpetuate the alienation and de-souling of the world which defines our Western culture. If psychotherapists, the modern-day custodians of soul care, are as fearful and rejecting of the ancient earth deities as is our culture, how can they possibly facilitate the healing of the deep soul-splitting wounds that our Judeo-Christian culture has chosen to sanctify?

Let me close with some reflections on the AIDS epidemic. What are the gods wanting that they have afflicted us with one of the most devastating sexually transmitted diseases in human history? Why have they chosen to launch their first attack on homosexuals? And why should this attack come so soon after

the gay community came out of hiding and fought so courageously to have their sexuality respected? One would have
expected the sexual gods to be pleased. Certainly Pan must
have been delighted to be freed to openly pursue his lusts after
so many centuries of imprisonment. But in view of what I have
been saying about the Pan/Nymph archetype, perhaps we dishonor Pan when sexuality habitually becomes too easy and
casual. We must never lose touch with the awesome terror that
always accompanies the sudden influx of Pan's lustful desire
for the elusive, fragile beauty of the Nymph.

Not for nothing has Christianity identified humankind's
carnal nature with Evil. The transformation of sexuality, which
I believe is the key to soul-making, is a process which requires
us to honor and celebrate all the gods so that we may develop
our capacity to contain the opposites. A poem by D. H.
Lawrence on his experience of soul is a suitable anthem for the
task of soul-making:[13]

> That I am I.
>
> That my soul is a dark forest.
>
> That my known self will never be
> more than a little clearing in the forest.
>
> That gods, strange gods, come forth
> from the forest into the clearing of
> my known self, and then go back.
>
> That I must have the courage to let
> them come and go.
>
> That I will never let mankind put
> anything over me, but that I will
> try always to recognize and to honor
> the gods in me and the gods in
> other men and women.

PART V

Addiction

Introduction

This thing of Darkness I acknowledge mine.

—Shakespeare

A MERICA WAS FOUNDED ON A VISION of the human being that says there is something in us and between us that transcends our earthly identities and the limits of our egos. Woven firmly throughout the American mystique, in historical themes such as "manifest destiny" and the "separation of church and state," is the belief that these ideals go beyond our blind adherence to religious dogmas or institutionalized government. When we look deeply at the American psyche, we see a spiritual foundation that has its own life.

We all carry a holy longing, a yearning to know the meaning of our lives, to have a connection with the transpersonal, to experience the spiritual dimension of human life, to return to our souls' divine origins. Spirituality is the art of creating union with something greater than ourselves, with a Higher Power. When too much of our potential is unlived and hidden in the unconscious, if we put too much emphasis on conscious attitudes and allow little room in our world view for the spiritual, our egos tend toward rigidity and shallowness. We suffer from mental sterility, daily existence becomes banal, and we are vulnerable to "possession" by the shadow. When the unconscious is cut off from consciousness, the unacknowl-edged shadow builds inside us as a counter-force screaming to be acknowledged. If not received voluntarily, it will assert itself more and more strongly.

The splitting away of those parts of us that we can't accept becomes the foundation for the shadow personality. This in turn produces a strong emotional charge in the unconscious, since the repressed contents are disturbing or negative emo-tions. All of this comes easily to us since the exclusion of emo-tion is deeply embedded in the American psyche; our national character, our cultural shadow, relies heavily on left-brain, thinking-dominated processes. But try as we might to cling to "reason," our strong feelings continue to seek expression. Driven by the cultural taboos against expressing our feelings, the emotional aspect of our lives will almost certainly ret-rogress and emerge, unexpectedly, as self-destructive behavior. While these behaviors may initially be driven by a desire to sat-isfy our needs for pleasure, spontaneity, and spiritual comfort, they eventually devolve into something quite the opposite—trance-like habits that play havoc with our lives.

If we look to literature, we find examples of the compen-satory nature of the shadow illustrated in the great stories. There is the legendary Dr. Faust, who understands only through his intellectual powers. Out of boredom with his limi-tations he makes a pact with the devil, Mephistopheles, and eventually deteriorates into a drunken dissipated soul. In Robert Louis Stevenson's story, *The Strange Case of Dr. Jekyll and Mr. Hyde,* a pathetically proper and pious Victorian gen-tleman releases his destructive shadow (Mr. Hyde, the "hid-den" monstrous side) through drug use.

In the film version of *Jekyll and Hyde,* Dr. Henry Jekyll says to his students, "The soul of man is not truly one but truly two." Because this inner split becomes too painful to contain within his rigid professional persona, Jekyll deludes himself into thinking that the two selves can be truly kept apart from one another. "How much freer the good in us would be," he says in the 1932 film. "What heights it might scale. And the so-called evil would fulfill itself and trouble us no more."[1]

In both of these cautionary tales, we are shown that if we fail to attend to the shadow side it can erupt and destroy the civilized side. In the end, as we know, Mr. Hyde destroys not only himself but his host, the "good" Dr. Jekyll. This is so often the case with addictive disorders. Initially, the addict is attracted to the high side of life, wants to fly free, elevated far above the drudgery of daily life. But he or she looks in the wrong places, and in the end these doomed efforts to embrace our higher nature produce just the opposite results.

We are creatures of habit, though some of our habits are worse than others. Our deep hunger and longing are not easily satisfied by reason. When it is not acknowledged, this hunger is often manifest in forms that degrade rather than nourish or elevate us. We may receive warnings, we might develop symptoms. Most likely, we will act out unconsciously—as if a force has taken us over—through compulsive, self-destructive behavior.

The list of habitual trance-like behaviors, and the substances by which we might seek to fill our spiritual and emotional emptiness, is nearly endless—food, sex, chemicals, intoxicants, gurus, relationships, prescription drugs, religion, and even personal development itself. The real danger is generally not in the substance or action itself but in the fact that those substances or activities cannot possibly fulfill the compelling human need for spiritual meaning. As long as we are willing to give our power over to such machinations, our needs only become exaggerated and distorted. When in the grips of such a fruitless pattern, we are harnessed to a seductive and deadly treadmill of life habits that saps our aliveness and deepens our despair.

Jung once said that the "craving for alcohol was the equivalent, on a low level, of the spiritual thirst of our being for wholeness . . . 'alcohol' in Latin is *spiritus*, and you use the same word for the highest religious experience as well as for the most depraving poison."[2] We must be cautious of symptom-based medical models for the treatment of addictive disorders. They tend to whitewash the dilemma and are really just outgrowths of the same problem they are intended to heal. To adequately address addictive behavior, we must never forget the underlying spiritual problem. The relative success of 12-step recovery programs, with their emphasis on conscious contact with a Higher Power, has shown that the ultimate sources for recovery are spiritual. The unity we are seeking requires awakening inner healing power through an encounter with the dark side.

Jacquelyn Small's essay, "Sacred Hunger: Shadow, Ecstacy, and Addiction," gives context to the shadow-spiritual problem of addiction. She views addiction as "untamed libido," shadow running out of control, craving to be understood. She suggests that healing from addiction can be achieved by transforming our excessive tendencies, by developing the discipline to look and listen to what is trying to emerge through the action of the addictive behavior. There is a message in this essay that speaks to us all, whether our addictions are life-threatening or relatively benign, a prescription for living our lives with greater spontaneity and the freedom to "fly" beyond the banal.

—J. A.

Sacred Hunger: Shadow, Ecstasy, and Addiction

JACQUELYN SMALL

Son of man, bathe yourself in the ocean of matter. . .
for it is that ocean which will raise you up to God.
—Teilhard de Chardin, *Hymn to the Universe*

Dualism Is in Our Nature

NEVER IN HUMAN HISTORY have we been free of the task of dealing with conflicting pairs of opposites, maneuvering between the shadow and the light. As creatures of the earth, we need both male and female to conceive a child; our religions warn of good and evil to guide an immature humanity. In this world we've been created under the biophysical influence of double-helix DNA. We carry the pattern for duality.

The "warring opposites," in whose midst we live, provoke us to continually function in an "either/or" mentality. The ongoing battle of right/wrong, win/lose, good/bad, should/shouldn't is incessant and consumes much of our emotional lives. The human tendency is to get lost in one side of the polarity, to remain resistant to the unwanted side, often in a state of innocent denial.

Dualism is in our nature. These opposites are what C. G. Jung called the "sparring partners." In some fashion, they represent every possible human dilemma. The struggles between the dark and light within us become the issues that often shake us to our core and force us to seek a higher way, or else become resigned and lost.

So here we are, with both a hidden dark shadow side that we deplore and refuse to own, and an ideal self-image we don for all to see. We approve of ourselves when we've been "good" and feel self-disgust when we're "bad." Until we recognize that these twin polar characters inhabit our one bodily form— and that they are one and the same creature—we're in grave trouble, forever in danger of losing touch with our soul.

For example, I really love helping people who are down and out, and know it is my life's work to do so; yet there are times when this service is tedious and quite unpleasant. To stay healthy myself, I must therefore have a container for the expression of this negative side of my feelings, rather than pretending I don't ever feel these things. Otherwise, this "dark side" will act out behind my own back, and one day I may be verbally abusive to a client or come home and kick my cat or yell at my son. The emotional energy I'm denying must have somewhere to go. And unfortunately, our negativity tends to land on those we love the most.

Or here's another "dark" story: A father has a very talented son, who represents all the successes in sports that the father had always dreamed of for himself. To see the son advance and win recognition may elicit mixed feelings in the dad of both pride in his son and a seething envy. If the dark side of his feelings are not acknowledged (at least to himself), he may become passive-aggressive and fail to show up at the occasion of his son's highest honor.

We think of this constant pull between this way and that way as something wrong with us that we're supposed to overcome; and though we try with all our might to be *only* positive, believing this is how we're all supposed to be, some Higher Power seems to have other plans for our mode of reaching heaven. This has always been the case, since the beginning of creation. Being positive only sounds like a good idea. Unfortunately, it never works. "All natures are good," said Dr. Jung, "yet just not good enough to prevent their badness from being equally obvious."[3]

When the tension of the opposites builds beyond our ability to handle it, the stress either wipes us out, or it "pops" the two poles into some new thing that unifies on a higher level. This is apparently how we grow. Psychologically, we live within a "tension point between the warring opposites" that performs an evolutionary function for consciousness: the two are spiraled into the higher holism and unified as one, and we see there is another way—a better way—to live. Love is one-pointed, and emanates from the Source as our pure nature. Love is the frequency of creation. Fear is the frequency of separation, and generates dualism.

Dualism, though as real as we feel it to be, is truly an illusion. The One is our single Source and is always three, not two. For there's no way to separate from the point where both sides originated. All pairs of opposites will have their unifying center, making a triangle instead of a polarity:

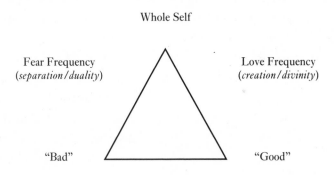

Whole Self

Fear Frequency
(*separation/duality*)

Love Frequency
(*creation/divinity*)

"Bad"

"Good"

The Law of Creativity has three parts, not two, since it emanates from the divine: thesis, antithesis, and synthesis—a yes, a no, and a resolution. But as we struggle through any creative process, there will always be a dimension of consciousness we experience as irreconcilable opposites; and there is a higher, more integrated dimension just beyond our reach, where the apparent dualities, no matter how extreme, will unite once we make this center point conscious. Therefore, to create anything at all we'll naturally have some chaos or negativity with which to contend. The antithesis part is what builds up steam, separates out what doesn't work, and fuels the fire that melts our rich "ingredients" into the one finished work of art. Without conflict, there can be no transformation. Light cannot be seen until it strikes an object. From the perspective of the Higher Self, the apparent opposites are always just two sides of the same issue.

The self is both the origin and the goal of our existence, the "organizing principle" or blueprint for a whole human being. Many do not accept the Self as real because we cannot quite get hold of it. The Self is not a physical "thing", it has *archetypal nature*. It is never seen in the outer world but is accessed introspectively and symbolically, through our dreams, fantasies, and inner images of wholeness. Archetypes are thematic representations that are similar in all *homo sapiens*. The Self is the central archetype, or organizing principle, that keeps pushing us instinctively toward the completion of our species. Jung believed that the archetypes are the mental/symbolic counterparts to the physical instincts—two poles of the same phenomenon—that are somehow connected. They seize our minds in the same autonomous manner as the instincts do, and take over our lives automatically in certain situations. No matter what culture we come from, we all have an "instinctual" drive to become fully realized. The completed Self is the *Imago Dei*, the image of the divine within each of us. We are "made in the image of God" (Gen. 1:27), cocreators by divine right.

Ecstasy and Addiction

MORE THAN ANYTHING ELSE, what puts the imprint of our God-nature on our lives is the power of *desire* within the soul. There is impetus within human nature moving us toward the sanctification of our desire nature. We are always seeking to merge with the divine.

What we've not realized is this: Through this feeling of "divine discontent," this constant seeking a greater identity, we eventually drive ourselves into a replica of our Ideal. Whenever we are moving in this forward direction, we are pleased with ourselves and life seems worth living, even during the hard times. We feel a deep sense of meaning and purpose in our existence and a kind of erotic gratification like that which accompanies all fulfilling affairs of the heart.

When we experience this high, we feel we are living in God and God is living in us, and we are in ecstasy. God's nature as desire and love comes toward us. And we—made in His image—become this desire and love ourselves.

Religious ecstasy has been part of human experience throughout the ages. It was the integral experience in the early Christian church. The ancient Greek Orthodox Church believed that God looks out through our eyes. Humans were seen as divine. To learn to embody and enact the themes of Life and Love personally was the equivalent of doing God's will. According to such early Christian theology, we were never meant to externalize an authority in the sky, but instead to learn to act creatively and morally under our own steam. Morality was thought of as the complete alignment of thought with the rapture of being alive.[4]

But this ecstatic state of consciousness always has been feared because it's so exotic and such a high energy state. We run from it to avoid becoming obsessed. Or we may find that, once it's tasted, we cannot live without it. On a deep unconscious level, many of us would prefer to never allow ourselves this intense rapture; to experience it and then lose it would be intolerable. We both fear and adore our passions and the delicious fruits of this earthy existence.

This sensual/emotional/feeling level of living is where many experience the deepest splits, imbalances, and confusions. And here is where we discover the deepest agent of neurotic pain and all the addiction disorders that carry us to the extremes. We are afraid to claim what truly gives us the most pleasure in life, to go for it in ways that really work, so we continually seek out substitutes for divine ecstasy. We fear if we had the real thing, we'd be consumed in the fires of passion and driven right out of our minds. Or, worse, that once attained, this ecstasy might become so "familiar" that it would lose its allure, and we'd be forever bored!

This incurable yearning toward wholeness is real. Today, even modern physics is realizing that our nature is divine. Humans are hybrid creatures made up of both spirit and matter, needing to live in both realms. We must learn to offer the world a way of approach that honors both the ego's desire to be holy and the soul's true delight at getting to be all-too-human.

Our inability to understand how to resolve these troublesome oppositions within us have led many an unsteady soul to literalize the yearning and to fall into the lure of addiction. And quite a treacherous road it is—one that nobody would ever *consciously* choose! It's so natural to love the sensuous pleasures and the feeling of being high. Yet these longings can get us into a lot of trouble.

There is a connection between the shadow's ways and our addictive nature, for each operates in the closets of denial and fear, repressing the passionate and "untamed" side of our nature. Even our lowliest shadow self has a purposeful and holy function. Falling all the way down to the bottom of an addiction and climbing up again turns out to be a most intriguing part of the Divine Plan for humanity. For who would best know about the activities of creation than the God who invented the game?

Can you get a sense of the conflict most of us feel within our desire nature? Rather than having to choose between the nonexistent "opposites," there is an alternative: thesis-antithesis resolves when we grasp and can live out the dance of divine ecstasy. This has always been the case, though most of us simply have not caught on.

Brugh Joy, teacher and medical metaphysician, has his students chant the maxim, "The light, the dark, no difference!" This simple awareness, when sacralized, holds the magic key. This is the stance we need to adopt if we are ever going to be whole. We are both the passionate "dark" and the calm, serene "light" side, and we must live within both our natures if we are ever to be whole.

But for most of us, it's a long way from here to there in our attitude toward the unconscious and disowned side of our nature, our despicable shadow self. A great deal of inner work must be employed before we can actually resolve this "devilish" split within our nature. A reframing of our biographies may be in order if we're ever going to succeed. Perhaps the following helps us in this regard.

If we start from the top down we will see how dualism originates within God's nature. A quick glance through the Old

Testament will cause any casual reader to see that God is not just a loving Father. His wrathful side was quite obvious and brought several of our ancestors to their knees! God was apparently not in touch with His "dark" intrinsic feminine nature. Dr. Jung was amazed at God's "peculiar behavior," at His lack of compassion for His creatures. "His light of love glows with a fierce dark heart. . ." said Jung, which caused him to conclude that ". . . fear of God should be considered the beginning of all wisdom."[5]

It appears that our struggle against God's ambivalent nature is our highest, all-encompassing dualism. Since we are "made in God's image," we must understand that His nature is an *antimony*, meaning a totality of inner opposites coexisting within one being, an indispensable condition for the dynamism required of a Creator! We, too, are an antimony. According to modern physics, in our subatomic foundations we function as both the particle and the wave. And our foundation is rooted in the Principle of Uncertainty.[6] So we are indeed sharing in our Creator's ambivalent nature. We are a vessel filled with divine conflict, as God's "oppositeness" has become embodied in us.

Integrating the shadow is the major and most difficult portion of our journey because the shadow, by definition, is unconsciousness. But instead of feeling like life's victims—that we're being "dragged along by fate" (Jung's phrase)—we can learn to do this inner work consciously, finding delight in our whole nature rather than denying a part of it, since the unconscious is going to make itself known anyway!

The Shadow: Symbol or Symptom

THE SHADOW IS AN ARCHETYPE, an *a priori* pattern residing in the "tissues" of our psyche. In its psychic reality it is a *sym-*

bol, an aspect of the Self. When we cannot find a way to work with our shadow through our dreams or other forms of inner work, it becomes a *symptom* in the world. The shadow begins in the lofty nature of God and descends all the way down the ladder into the hellish worlds to become "the devil."

On the archetypal level, every symbol has a dual nature which can manifest either negatively or positively in our dreams or outer life. The Cross, the Swastika, the Fish, the Great Mother, the Dark Lover, the Child, the Feminine, the Moon, the Earth, the Magician: each has a two-way meaning. We are both attracted and repelled, helped and harmed, by the very same symbols.

As a symptom in our lives, the shadow can be quite troublesome. According to Jungian Marie-Louise von Franz, the shadow takes the form of laziness, greed, envy, jealousy, the desire for prestige, aggressions, and similar "tormenting spirits."[7] When we ignore our shadow, it is like opening a door and allowing negative powers such as wrath, hatred, envy, lechery, or faint-heartedness to step in. In the olden days, we spoke of possession by demons or bad spirits. Addiction can be viewed as the shadow running out of control, as "untamed libido." Because it is so despised, the shadow can never give us its true gifts, the truth of our denied side. The shadow is the addicted part that is craving conscious expression in order to be understood and to connect with the civilized part so that appropriate social boundaries can be established.

We don't just *manage* our libido, we can transform it. We must work on assimilating the positive quality that is trying to emerge from untamed libido. This is how we view healing from addiction in our work. Instead of attempting to kill it by controlling our urges toward excess, we offer methods that enable the client or participant to get in touch with the feelings and images behind the excessive tendency. There we will access the archetypal pattern that has been activated in the addictive behavior and we can gain clues as to what is trying to emerge. It may be a god, a spirit, a demon, a complex, or processes closer to our Source, our wholeness.

Once accessed, we can turn this energy in a positive direction and see what unfolds as a hidden soul quality, talent, or desire which supports the emergence of the real Self. Some of these patterns enhance our lives, while others may bring great ordeals. This type of inner work provides an opportunity for us not only to advance personally; it contributes to collective evolution as one Humanity.

In shadow work, for instance, just to view your dark side as wounded from your biological abuse could dampen and block a person at an egoistic level. Victimization would be the result. Symbolically, if your shadow can become a spiritual opponent or warrior, a sparring partner for your evolution, your dark partner then becomes a constant reminder of the potential dangers along your path—such as overreaction or unconsciousness. This symbolization process deepens our understanding of the principle of "warring opposites" that governs concrete reality.

To think of our addictive shadow as only a bad symptom is limiting and fails to utilize its sacred transformational power as a symbol. Jung's interpretation of Jesus' message to Nicodemus about being born twice (John 3: 3–7) was this: "If you think materialistically, you'll be an ego. If you think symbolically, you'll become spirit." In other words, do not think "carnally" about your shadow nature or you will be filled with low self-esteem and self-loathing. But think symbolically and archetypally and you will transform your shadow, and thus become transformed yourself by assimilating the opposites within you. Jung describes this process as the "transcendent function," mediating the opposites and facilitating a transition from one psychological attitude or condition to another.

On our way to consciousness from the collective unconscious there will always be certain aspects of our nature that are "unlit" and will pop out, lopsided and ill-equipped to handle the light, undeveloped qualities that are undifferentiated and therefore unusable by our conscious personalities. At first, these are just impulses, not tamed at all. We often judge these uncivilized parts severely as bad or wrong, when, in fact, they simply must come up for air if they are ever going to become usable capacities.

If one side of us gets starved and we are suffering because of it, a compulsion is created to mask what is missing. This can lead to the chronic dysfunction of addictive behavior and obsessive attachments. Sometimes the shadow element can get really out of hand, moving too far into obsession: fanaticism, one-sided bigotry, dogmatic convictions ("my way is the only way"), compulsive over-activity; we can easily become a wind-up toy gone berserk, stuck banging up against a wall.

Whatever we get hooked on will get us every time. It is our nature to create a path of return to wholeness when we get this far off the mark in one-sidedness. The psyche will self-regulate and bring the other side of the polarity into play. This can mean a bottoming-out for the addict, a collapse for the compulsive doer, alienation, depression, and dissociation for the self-righteous zealot, or tragic consequences for anyone.

So trying to regulate some part of ourselves we see as "wicked," "immoral," or "wrong" can cause us great troubles, and can produce a regressed, often barbaric backlash. As long as the denied side remains unacknowledged and unexpressed, it can potentially explode the shadowy emotions that stew in denial, repression, self-hatred, and misunderstanding. The shadow grows to such potency because it has been denied recognition as a legitimate part. Anytime we get too one-sided on any issue of any sort, we are in for a rude awakening.

Enantiodromia: The Divine Adjuster

WHEN SOME EXTREME PSYCHOLOGICAL STATE runs to the end of its potential in one direction, it reverts to its other side. A great psychological law is at work. At some point, all human one-sidedness goes over to its opposite in order to make conscious the unlived part. Since our created nature is dualistic, everything in our nature must have its opposite. Therefore, if we insist on being lopsided about anything at all, we are guaranteed a surprise. One fateful day the inner Self suddenly says "Time's up! You've learned all you need to know from this." The compensatory function of the unconscious psyche has kicked in; now everything shifts. And we're forced to tumble all the way to the other side of our nature—to the part that's being ignored, disowned, or utterly denied. Goodness can turn into evil, happiness to unhappiness. The masquerade of a perfect couple who never fights shifts to a nasty divorce and custody battle. An exaggerated spirituality reverts to basic instincts. This explains how a TV evangelist preacher who screams at us about "the sins of the flesh" finds himself in the arms of a prostitute.

When there are gaps in our willingness to see and own any piece of ourselves, we can know for certain that the unconscious mind will compensate for this deficit and throw up an image or an actual experience to call it out. Jung called this process of shifting to the opposite extreme by its Latin name, *enantiodromia*, literally, running in the opposite direction. It is a psychological principle first described by the Roman Heraclitus; it means that sooner or later everything turns into its opposite. Jung felt this to be ". . . the principle which governs all cycles of natural life, from the smallest to the greatest."[8] He said that recognizing the inevitability of enantiodromic change helped him to anticipate psychic movement.

The inherent enantiodromia in the workings of the human psyche continually leads us to the shadow. If you notice that someone is always good, always smiling, always anything, you will know that the shadow is hiding in what is not being expressed.

To live a transformative life and avoid the enantiodromatic pendulum, one must find that place of tension—as much as one can stand—and learn to live there, right at the "zero-point," the exact middle between opposites, not at either pole, but in acceptance of both sides at once. Abraham Maslow called this "dichotomy transcending." We find the balance between work/play, selfish/ unselfish, childish/mature. We learn to "pull into shape" something new emerging on the periphery, while holding steady.

When people walk around in a state of "pretend equilibrium," however, they are sleepwalking. Balancing the tension between opposites may *appear* as equilibrium but it's really a pleasurable state of tension instead. The unhealthy addict misuses this tension by running from it, or getting hooked on either extreme. The healthy, creative person, on the other hand, utilizes this tension for the precipitation of talents and the making of dreams. This transmutation of energy, from blocked and denied to openly expressed, is how our shadow heals and becomes an active and recognized partner in our process of co-creation. Our passions and true calling merge.

For us to become consciously creative, we must bear up under our own inner contradictions. Consciousness flourishes through contrasts—by separating out figure from ground. But when we don't get the point, the psyche sets up a different way to present the discrepancy. Our errors then, and the obstacles along our path, become great gifts. If becoming conscious is our goal, this may be the only way we can learn. Once something is made conscious, it settles back into the pleroma of oneness—into the implicate order of reality—only now with an acquired sense of self-reflection.

Making Your Shadow's Acquaintance

TO BECOME CONSCIOUS OF YOUR SHADOW means first to recognize the dark sides of your personality as real and present, to realize that we *all* have an autonomous emotional nature of obsessions and possessiveness to some degree. The reason most people cannot recognize their shadow is because these inferior personality traits, unconscious and unformed, are primarily *emotional* in nature. These feelings are largely autonomous and difficult to identify and control. The shadow stands behind all these strong feelings.

But we can't actually see one consistent entity who plays the shadow's role. Its form will change, sometimes from moment to moment, depending upon which issue is up. The shadow is undifferentiated emotional energy that has never taken form. And we fear it because it's unknown. Its mysterious powers frighten us. Yet it holds the key to our earthy dynamism. In his teachings, Jung warns over and over that we cannot know the shadow intellectually; its energies must form in our lives so that we can "see" it, or in our minds during inner work.

This dark and mysterious side of our nature is actually the numinous "glow" of our divine and wholistic nature. This is the treasured part of us that comes with such bad press, we've even tried to completely throw it out of our personalities. And yes, it's the part we prefer to project out onto others and then "spit upon." This is especially true of many who consider themselves spiritual, or highly evolved—which is, of course, a drastic mistake.

Until made conscious, the shadow causes us to act in ways that create catastrophe or explosions of emotionalism. It stands there on the threshold of our unconscious mind, reflecting back to us our blind side. We must learn to embrace the shadow without trying to win it over. It is our teacher. We are often not able to hear the more kindly offerings of our friends, consequently, it must pop out from time to time and remind us from inside. When we try to deny the shadow it multiplies. When instead we choose to invite it in, we gain stability and expand consciousness, losing our self-righteousness, and becoming flexible, less defended, more balanced.

When we can stand on someone's blind side without judgment, we are aiding that person. Often, it requires the help of a good therapist or psycho-spiritual group to explore the shadow's domain. If you're brave enough to undergo the task alone, confident in your ego strength, you can ask your shadow to show itself to you through inner work. You can put on some music that is emotionally evocative, and gently call it out. You can go within and dialogue with your shadow, or keep a "shadow journal," write letters to it, have it answer you. Tell it you will accept it, no matter what, that you will hold it in your heart if it will reveal itself.

The Shadow as the Addicted "Needy" Self

CLOSER TO OUR ORDINARY LIVES, we can see how the process of addiction works for our personal development.

First, we begin doing something quite natural—enjoying a bottle of beer, falling madly in love, getting all jazzed and over-invested in some exciting project, buying too many expensive things, bragging excessively about ourselves, even to the point of lying. A few months down the road, we notice we're engaged in this favored behavior more and more often, even obsessively. Now it's beginning to consume our time and our mental energies. Next thing we know, we are making sacrifices in our lives in order to maintain a steady flow of this "whatever" that's so turning us on.

Then, one day in sheer disgust, we realize that "too much" is never going to be enough, and we sink into a terrifying despair. We see (or someone close to us observes) that we're making a total fool of ourselves attempting to gratify some hunger, but too late: it has already happened. The damage is done. People are moving away from us, and our lives are shutting down. We are now being confronted: verbally by those who love us, and experientially by our life. Our self-esteem, our hopes, visions, and dreams begin to die and so do we. The curtain closes and life feels completely undone. We've hit bottom.

It is as though we'd been living at the tension point of a rubber band stretched to the maximum. And suddenly, from this place of greatest strain, an inner Someone just abruptly lets go and we fall into a completely uncivilized state of chaos. We go completely unconscious and act out our greatest fear. We actually can see the shadow in this active addictive behavior—it's all one dance.

Outwardly, we've completely humiliated ourselves. Our persona has crashed and burned, we're left wide open, raw, and vulnerable—completely "seen." We've alienated most of our outer life. And here lies the blessing: *Now there is nothing between us and the root consciousness whence we've sprung.* All defenses have dropped away, and we are utterly finished as the one that we once were. We've run an identity all the way to its finish line. We've hit the edge of the frame around the self-image we'd carried for all the world to see. From these depths, a new life begins, though it certainly does not feel like new life while we're in the midst of hitting bottom.

Addictions of any sort perfectly replicate the process of projecting outwardly our dark side, eventually forcing us at some point to undergo a rude awakening. Codependence, the relationship addiction, is an example with which most of us can identify. It appears to be the shadow side of our love nature. I called codependence "needy love" in my book *Awakening in Time:*[9] "Needy love is how the shadow dances." Many of you know intuitively what I mean, how the shadow moves about in our relationships masquerading needs as love.

For most of my adult life I have studied, theoretically and experientially, the nature of addiction, most especially in the area of relationships. Both personally and professionally, I've become familiar with the bittersweet essence of addiction, and I continue to be fascinated by its circuitous way of shattering *and* also transforming many a life, sometimes the lives of entire families.

Once, in a group setting during an intensive month-long workshop, we asked a group of students (several of whom were in recovery from chemical addiction and codependency) to go into a meditative trance state and ask their Higher Power to tell them the meaning and sacred purpose of addiction, our "shadow disease of the extremes." Here is a sampling of the messages that came from the Higher Self:

- Addiction is a confusion within the desire nature—a misplacing of focus.

- Addiction is blocked creative expression.

- Addiction is a way to materialize attachment and make the pain so evident that humanity has to deal with it.

- Addiction is the dark side of the love force—a transitory pleasure becomes a god; worship in the wrong direction.

- Addiction is focusing intently on something that no longer has meaning.

- Addiction is the purification of our desire nature, a transitory disease while changing levels of consciousness.

- Addiction is a polarizing force which gives us enough "push" to pop through in surrender.

- Addiction is a holding pattern, a way to stay stuck and avoid the tasks at the next emerging level of consciousness.

- Addictions are the scars that humankind has against knowing its own nature.

- The process of addiction raises the kundalini energy of the earth.

- Addiction is blocked light.

- Addiction is the factor that determines whether we evolve or simply recur.

In all of these messages about addiction, you can sense a sacred function, an evolutionary purpose. In fact, I see within the addict's frenetic search to find the "too much" that would feel like enough, the key to our evolution.

In the world of dualism, we must unfortunately learn what *is* through experiencing what is *not*. In a state of addiction, we believe we are in need of something external to complete us, give us our life. Addictions are the negative side of our desire nature and show us who we're *not*. This is the divine shadow at work!

The process of addiction must include a psycho-spiritual context in order for healing to occur. Both the ego's biography and family of origin issues must be addressed, as well as the spiritual hunger underneath all the outward searching. It is this yearning to become our highest Self that eventually triggers healing. Hardly ever does a human being know how to go about this process of becoming the archetypal human—which is divine—in a healthy and life-giving manner. Many flounder on the path of Self-realization, often through a shadow entanglement of some sort. And perhaps this is our plight: Without a philosophy that honors the principles of wholeness of both our psychological and spiritual parts, we spiritual beings in human form cannot find an ambiance for the sacred and essential healing work that we require. The process of addiction and recovery is a spiritual path. It will eventually lead us to our Source. We'll eventually hit bottom with any type of serious addiction, since nothing outside us can ever really fulfill us. When we lose the image of what (who) we are longing to become, we are lost. Once on the path of recovery, we begin to rise up to new heights of understanding our nature. We see that we were looking for our life, but in the wrong direction.

We're all in need of healing, not from just one or two uncomplicated symptoms, but from having been caught in the throes of the paradoxical and alluring human condition. As bioenergetic analyst John Conger states: "The purpose of the shadow is to provide the human soul with the opposition and tension to develop a tough inner resolve and determination to clarify through the challenge of the opposites."[10]

The Roots of Our Emotional Distress

AS WE STUDY THE LEVELS OF HUMAN UNFOLDMENT, we see clearly how our dysfunctional addictive patterns developed during our early years as a defense against the treatment to which many of us were subjected. But first I want to point out that our learning process doesn't begin when we land on the delivery table after birth; our first schoolroom is our mother's womb. For those of you interested in this statement, you might want to explore the works of Dr. Stanislav Grof and the emerging field of perinatal psychology, exemplified by work such as Dr. Thomas Verny's remarkable book, *Secret Life of the Unborn Child.*[11] These researchers are discovering that while we are still unborn and pre-verbal, our organ of information-gathering is not the intellect, but our whole selves—physical sensations, feelings, and intuitive perceptions. We learn through *experiential data.* And, unfortunately, this kind of wholistic learning is the hardest to later correct, because the learning has been imprinted throughout our being, in our very cells.

Once we are born, the problems begin to multiply. Parents who need their children emotionally for a sense of worthiness or ego strength demand unrealistic behavior from their tiny offspring; they may expect them to be perfect and always to shine, exemplifying to others the supposed values and worth of the family. As a child abuse caseworker, I saw cases where children less than 18 months old had learned to eat every bite of their food without spilling a drop; otherwise, they knew they'd be knocked across the room. I also saw cases where children lived amidst so much emotional drama, they learned from their grown-up family members that fighting and half-killing one another can lead to making up romantically, or to passionate lovemaking. An unchecked shadow had hold of the family dynamics, making its members dysfunctional carriers of these patterns into their subsequent family involvements.

Children in alcoholic families learned from the addict how to self-medicate and escape through substances; they are taught by the co-alcoholic how to control and manipulate. Others may have grown up with parents who had troubled marriages, where one parent may have turned to the child for nurturing and support, creating a syndrome of emotional incest. Or some parents sexually abused their children, leaving them with deep emotional scars and seriously distorted messages about sexuality and love. Many have grown up with such terribly damaging storylines, everything from "you're here for my pleasure" to "drink or drug till you feel numb."

In my experience as a therapist, I've found a direct correlation between children who were molested by a relative or significant other and a later addiction to sex and/or romantic love. We've also found correlation between eating disorders and emotional or sensual/erotic confusion, as food can become symbolic for "giving and getting" emotional/sensual gratification, as well as a way to have control over one's own body. Many suffering from anorexia or bulimia have been erotically mishandled or sexually or emotionally abused when very young and innocent. As a result, their attitude toward sexuality and sensuality is founded in imbalance, ambivalence, and a confusion between sexual feelings and parental love.

As you are reading this, some feelings may be coming up for you; this may be stirring up some important aspects of your own early childhood situation; or you may be seeing some of the ways you've been confused about your sexual and/or feeling nature. Please know that if this is happening, it may be the beginning of a healing process—a recognition. A part of your shadow is revealing itself so it can be seen, felt through, and healed. Once you make any of these contents conscious, you'll feel a need to go on and release the old hurts and misunderstandings that are still living in your body. You may want to seek out a good friend or safe therapist to help you give expression to these emerging issues. The shadow can only integrate by becoming known. But remember, you are always greater than any condition or negative experience to which you've been subjected.

Because feeling states function dynamically, our emotions cannot simply be talked about; they must be felt through to a release. Shadow work has to be experiential work. We need to revisit our past through processes such as breathwork, psychodrama, emotional-release work, guided imagery, deep body work, music/movement therapy, and other such methods that access and allow expression of the pent-up feelings in our cells and in our hearts that we're trying to ignore. In a setting where we feel safe and supported, painful feelings must be emptied out, like squeezing toothpaste out of a tube. Once released, we can see our life situations with the pristine clarity that naturally ensues when we live from center.

As a result of these early emotional insults to your evolving soul, you may have a shadow who's a junkie for highs. When the urge to give birth to something new strikes, a compulsive hunger is aroused and you may turn toward addictive pleasure-seeking. This intense longing for a turn on ignites you like a flame, and mistakenly, you begin to look outside yourself toward the world's glamour and titillating materialistic pleasures, yearning to be consumed.

In romantic relationships, the shadow will take on the roles that play out these melodramas and keep us away from our true emotions: the Don Juan, the seductive manipulator, the tease, the femme fatale, the hysteric. These subpersonalities thus become the shadow's pleasure-seekers. If your emotional body is addicted to extremes, you can become a fertile ground for the strong emotions of jealousy, clinging, possessiveness, and hatred. We become addicted to the need to feel special and turned on. When we don't get our fix, we feel dead and go sullen, turn in on ourselves, or act out shadowy behaviors.

Struggling through life seeking highs or "looking for love in all the wrong places" is often the loneliest game in town. There is constant rejection, lack of intimacy, competitiveness, and the need to be eternally youthful, sexy, and sensational—a breeding ground for chemical addiction and codependence. Issues concerning commitment, faithfulness, integrity, trust, and intimacy are trampled in this mirage. There is very little security or love that can emerge until these feeling-state imbalances and illusions are put to rest, or at least made conscious. This is the shadow's playground!

The Sacred Hunger

WE OFTEN CONFUSE OUR SEXUAL/RELATIONAL NATURE with the urge for transcendence and expression of creativity. Our human passion center is the place within our consciousness where we learn to merge with life and others with enthusiasm and a desire for intensity. The urge to be turned on and delighted—to feel high—is our natural feeling-tone. Devoid of these energies, we would have no interests or ability to be creative, for we'd never be attracted to anything we'd want to manifest.

We all know that in sexuality we procreate. But we may not have realized that artists and inventors are doing the very same thing: They, too, merge with something other than themselves (a canvas, a piece of clay) and create an offspring—a masterpiece. Lovers are the artists of Self-creation, and artists are true lovers of life. To our unconscious instinctive mind, the process is the same.

Allurement draws us all to our destiny by pulling us toward the people and projects representative of our true expression. This is the sacred Law of Attraction in operation in our lives, which functions in this world through its essential qualities of love and wisdom.

Until we become conscious of how we are misusing these powers of allurement and attraction—which are actually the magnetic and binding forces of love—we will search out other people and external things as substitutes for our inner Beloved. We lay our expectation on these others that they will turn us on. In our addiction, we've forgotten that turning on is an *inside* job, that we're either on or we're off, having to do with *our own* process, and never someone else's. It's the way we confuse outer stimuli for the inner yearning to be fascinated, creative, expressive, and transforming in life. We've become out of touch with our real Self, our true Beloved. And so we fall in love with "drama kings and queens," the shadow's playmates, or we get hooked on passion and intensity. What we are really seeking is not these "contents" at all, but the rapture of being alive, ecstasy. It is a sacred hunger.

Living within the uncertainty and tolerating the ambiguity of our nature is the goal of all true healing processes. That which redeems us evolves from our own pure nature—sexual instincts, the urges toward connectedness, the craving for depth and rapture. These cravings are natural to our species. Our human energies must be transformed along the lines of their natural designs. That which saves us physically provides the springboard for that which eventually saves us spiritually—the goal is to become fully one's Self.

Today's Task

TODAY, BECAUSE WE ARE ENDING a great cycle at the closing of an Age, it's not just hard core addicts who seek recovery in their personal lives; right now, the personal and universal are merging. *All* Humanity as one soul must enter into the Great Unknown, and learn to simply "let go and let God." We're not just ending one little personal cycle; our entire world view is shifting. This means that *all* our storylines and beliefs are currently up for an all-encompassing evaluation.

We've gotten stuck in a lopsided, ego-based, outer-focused way of viewing the healing process—one ruled by materialistic leadership, big business, insurance companies, and "managed care." So now a "global enantiodromia" is setting in all around us, to hopefully lead us to the other side. Many mental health and addictions treatment programs are currently failing in this country because they've hit the end of the road and completed a cycle. It's time to move on. We are being called to take a new look at what we value, at what we already know in our hearts and, most importantly, at what we desire our future to be.

Right now, in our world, *implosion* is how the shadow is at work in the collective. It is "cooking." We no longer have anyone to scapegoat; there is nowhere to go to keep our denial mechanism intact. So it's important now to bring a psychospiritual understanding to the world so we can integrate our emergent shadow.

Shadow work and addiction recovery are keys to our continuity as human souls. For whatever we make conscious, we have power over its use; but whatever remains unconscious has the power to do us in. And as we uncover the Self who resides within us at the core of our being, we're in for a great surprise: We'll find that coming clean doesn't mean we have to relinquish our passionate nature. Quite the opposite: Uniting with the Self is the ultimate high, a reunion with our one true Beloved of the soul—and this time, in human form.

PART VI

Money

Introduction

In the last resort
there is no good that cannot
produce evil
and no evil that cannot
produce good.

—C. G. Jung

What's money? A man is a success if he gets up in the
morning and goes to bed at night and in between does
what he wants to do.

—Bob Dylan

Being Alive

The only reason for living is being fully alive;
and you can't be fully alive if you are crushed by secret fear,
and bullied with the threat: Get money or eat dirt!—
and forced to do a thousand mean things
meaner than your nature,
and forced to clutch on to possessions
in the hope they'll make you feel safe,
and forced to watch everyone that comes near you,
lest they've come to do you down.

Without a bit of common trust in one another,
we can't live.
In the end, we go insane.
It is the penalty of fear and meanness,
being meaner than our natures.

To be alive, you've got to feel a generous flow,
and under a competitive system that is impossible, really.
The world is waiting for a great new movement of
    generosity,
or for a great wave of death.

We must change the system, and make living free to all men,
or we must see men die, and then die ourselves.
                                        —D. H. Lawrence, 1929[1]

AMERICANS LIVE TODAY IN A WORLD that is economically determined. The modern world of commerce continues to develop on a fantasy of growth, expanding exponen-
tially. It has become a strange new world, one of shape-shifters
and paper-shufflers who "make money" without ever lifting a
finger or exchanging a glance. Global competitive markets,
multinational corporations, international bankers and stock
market brokers, transnational commodities markets—all com-
pete and thrive in a world of speculative paper capital that
seems absurdly remote from the reality of our everyday lives.
We don't know how to measure the value of money, since it is
no longer based on a reliable gold standard, except in the language of supply and demand. We are only too aware that
money's value is manipulated by bureaucrats, bankers, and an
assortment of economic wizards and schemers.

There seems to be an ethical vacuum around the complex
theme of money. It is ironic that prosperity continues to flour-
ish world-wide, riding the waves of inflationary and deflation-
ary cycles, even as millions of human beings are starving to
death each year. The earth is depleted of its non-replenishable
resources to fuel the engines of progress, while hundreds of
species annually are threatened with extinction by pollution

and loss of habitat. And the American largesse, which affords many the highest personal standard of living in human history, today cannot afford the burden of its underprivileged classes. This is no small paradox.

Long ago in the course of human events, money became profane. Once, it was a sacred tool that connected human activity to the transcendent:

> The story of money, like the myth of the Holy Grail, is a tale of the corruption of ancient ideals of virtue by slowly corroding evil. . . The first form of money was shared food, which for many centuries preceded the evolution of coinage. Coinage . . . had the same significance as the Grail—that of a sacred relic symbolizing a holy meal among a loyal fellowship . . . Money, in our culture, originated in an identical manner as the Holy Grail, in a ritual communion meal in which the shared food symbolized mutual dedication among the communicants. Our money began as a religious symbol . . . as a symbol of man's soul.[2]

Today we suffer from mythlessness. We lack a viable, functioning collective myth to connect us to the transpersonal dimension of the soul. We need visionary thinking that could take us beyond the purely physical basis of economic reality. Our sacramental coins have themselves been transformed into a new kind of god, the Almighty Dollar. What are the forces now at work in American culture that bring us to serve such a false, materialistic principle? Is it true that money—or more precisely, the "love of money"—is the root of all evil? What *has* value any more, one might ask? We human beings have always been in a mess. But is it getting worse? Is money itself the corrupting influence on our values?

Our nation has deep roots in the stoic Puritan ethic, an attitude that has made the virtues of hard work and perseverance as American as the flag and the bald eagle. The shadow of our Puritanical roots may very well be a greedy, insatiable god in the American psyche, a cruel and amoral daimon that demands all the rewards of our efforts, and then some. Materialism is the new sacrament. But the painted cakes of materialism do not satisfy hunger.

Money is a commodity, a necessity, and getting it has become an inordinately high priority in American life. All of us are conscious of the governmental and institutional manipulation of money, and we each have some fear about the forces that can come down upon us if we don't have money. There is tremendous communal shame about not having enough money, of never feeling good enough. We may be hard-working and sincere, poor but honest, and still not be immune from the suffering and low self-worth. The finite nature of money compels us, influences our sense of personal worth. The old saw that "you can't take it with you" seems somewhat irrelevant; more to the point is the fact that most of us don't feel worthy because we can't get ahead of the money problem. The increasing criminalization of our society is a direct result of this shadow side of money. Addiction may be one side of the drug trafficking in our country, for example, but there are great sums of money to be made in this illicit activity. Most criminal acts, both white collar and the garden variety, are financially motivated.

Perhaps the shadow of money in America is the fear and distress it produces, *both the fear of not having it and the fear of having it,* and that we won't meet our needs either way. It's more shameful to not have money than to have it and hoard it; not having it is proof of one's unworthiness, proof of one's guilt, a punishment by an unjust god. One of the chief reasons that people cannot live within their means is the embarrassment caused by not having the symbols of affluence. The manipulation of money on a personal level, the vicious cycle of credit card spending and debt, is a new symptom of the shadow of money.

We rarely choose to admit that financial considerations drive us or determine our decisions. But to sneer at money and to see it as crass filthy lucre is to deny its essential reality. The cost of living our civilized American lifestyles has grown so much in recent decades that fewer households can exist on single incomes. Many of the decisions we have to make in the course of daily life are based on cost, on the availability of funds, on values strictly monetary. Money rules our career choices, a major factor that determines the quality of our lifestyles. The materialistic promise of the American dream seems to have tarnished; "Small is beautiful" was never before a part of our collective aesthetic. For many Americans, the green motto of "volunteer simplicity" is neither voluntary nor simple.

Today money is no longer associated with spirit, soul, or gold. Yet there is a great deal of soul in money: suffering about it, secrecy around it, fantasies about it, fascination with it, hopes attached to it, energy contained in it. We connect money to the life-force; we feel good—sometimes even omipotent—when we have it. We feel dejected and lifeless when we don't. Money is one of the great projection carriers for soul, according to Swiss psychiatrist, Adolf Guggenbühl-Craig. He says that we need to see that we project our souls onto money, to realize and reflect on the symbolic relationship we have with it, and thus be able to live out the projections with individual meaning: "The aim is to live our projections, hold on to them, while seeing that they are projections, that most of our deeds are only symbolic rituals . . . Projections of soul onto money have advantages over other projections. What we experience through money, what we project on money, is so clearly a projection . . . so easy to recognize—much easier than projections of soul on relationships or art."[3]

Robert Sardello gives us the depth and breadth of the money problem in his essay, "The Moneyed Society." To say that money is shadowy is stating the obvious; Sardello wants us to connect soul and money. Rather than taking on the shadow of money in American society as just another problem to fix, Sardello takes a phenomenological approach, reinvesting story and wit into our somewhat dulled sense of the meaning of money, with the hope of helping us reflect on the way money actually acts, not on the way we think it acts.

—J. A.

The Moneyed Society

ROBERT J. SARDELLO

W E LIVE IN AN ECONOMIC WORLD. Money has become the epistemology of our age—the focal point of our lives. It is what makes things happen. Our daily lives seem to revolve around it. Everything within us would like to deny that this is so, but the Almighty Dollar has quite clearly taken command of all our lives. And like the shadow that hides in the darkness of denial, the role that money plays in our lives gains impetus the more we try to hide it. In many respects, our other values are in bankruptcy, giving money the power of a sacred deity, demanding our attention, threatening to punish us if we fail to regularly express our daily devotion and honor its laws.

Economics, once believed to be the discipline that would civilize the monster, no longer persuades money to behave. All the money systems in the world have not been enough to make the beast lie down and be quiet, or sit up and do tricks for us. At best, economics appears to have become a money neurosis, a symptom of a problem rather than a viable methodology for finding a solution. As we suspected all along, the economists' scientific mask has proved to have little real substance behind it. And if we look honestly at the national debt we begin to suspect that most of our economists' efforts now revolve around maintaining the neurosis. As if hypnotized by the specter of the Almighty Dollar itself, we perhaps should be asking ourselves if we're colluding in the protection of a collective shadow that is eating us all alive.

Given the role money now takes in our lives, it is probably no surprise that the "science" of economics shares the language of psychopathology—inflation, depression, lows and highs, slumps and peaks, investments, losses. Similarly, like William Butler Yeats' rough beast "stumbling toward Bethlehem to be born," the economy stumbles along, caught up in endless manipulations, acting stimulated or depressed, drawing attention to itself, egotistically unaware of its own soul. Economists, brokers, accountants, financiers, all of them assisted by lawyers, have become the high priests of the money cult, performing endless rituals and chantings to harness the power of money to serve their own purposes.

Money, says Norman O. Brown, is the soul of the world. What an extraordinary statement! Money animates the world, he would have us believe. It is the life source—or at least appears to be! It might be better to admit from the outset that money is Almighty; stop trying to figure out ways to control it. Start looking for ways to revive our imagination for money.

When I speak of money, I am referring not to monetary theory but to money in its most tangible form, how we experience it in our daily lives, as pennies, nickels, dimes, quarters, and dollar bills. If we start here, maybe we'll find it therapeutic, like working with all the little matters that one brings into the therapist's room, instead of taking on the big textbook theories.

One standard definition calls money in this form—coins and bills—a condensation of value, a sign of wealth and a medium of exchange. If this is true, I want to listen to this message for its psychological implications, its stories and resonances. To do so loosens the hold of money as a *quantity* in our lives, and hopefully can help release the *qualities* of money, stimulating our imaginations.

Money as the Condensation of Value

THE WORD "CONDENSATION" SPEAKS to both the poet and the psychologist. In poetry, for example, the images the writer evokes with words are *condensations* of the qualities of the world. Carefully crafted, these images compress complex meanings into a few simple phrases. In psychology, our dream images are *condensation* of the qualities of the psychic world. Condensation, then, is at one and the same time a poetic and psychological concept.

Through money we remember our dead heroes, the ancestors of this land, who stood for and brought value into the community, often at the price of their own lives. The memories of their deeds are condensed in our money, making the energy, aspirations, and achievements of past heroes available to us on a daily basis, for a continuing transformation of the world, greening our hopes for the future. Through the face of the five-dollar bill, we remember Abraham Lincoln. Through the currency bearing his image, we can imagine the resounding words of the Gettysburg Address, smell the gun smoke and hear the cannon fire of the Civil War. We can feel the wounds of internal dissension—and anticipate the coming of Emancipation. On the other side of the bill, we are taken deeply into the Lincoln heritage. There we find and image of the Lincoln Memorial in Washington, D.C., in the architecture of an ancient Greek temple—making a new connection with the origins of the Western tradition. Lincoln, seated under thirty-six Doric columns, holds his arms firmly upon the arms of the chair, beneath which are two bundles of rods bound together—an ancient Roman symbol for political unity. There our hero rests, framed by two sprays of wheat, images of the goddess of Earth. On the steps in front of the memorial are tripods holding bowls—*patera*, Roman bowls used to hold the sacrifices offered to the gods, food from a public feast honoring the deeds of a hero.

If money memorializes our heroes, then perhaps we need to better understand the relationships between heroic deed, money, and the community. As tokens memorializing our heroes, money brings together the values inherent in the city, the land, the fruits of the earth, the necessity for sacrifice and the heroic deed. We all too readily take for granted the ritual act between one person and another, where a bit of green paper or a few metal coins are transformed into the object of a desire.

The background making this transaction ritual possible goes all but unnoticed, until suddenly it is quite clear that we've become inflated with our own sense of worth. The imagination associated with money is governed by neither government nor individuals. That imagination is governed by the formative vision of those ancestors circulating in our midst—Abraham Lincoln, George Washington, Lady Liberty, Alexander Hamilton, Susan B. Anthony, and all the rest. When we start measuring the value of money independent of the actions of our heroes, we are plagued by cycles of inflation and depression—all of which were states of the human soul long before they became notations on an accountant's ledger. When we look very closely, we discover that the rise and fall of the worth of money serves as an index of the acuity of our collective memory. There are two sides to every coin, we are told; one side turns toward and values the memories condensed in the imagery of our ancestors, while the other turns outward, valuing the world. The distance between them is paper thin.

Money's heroic qualities, giving power to the imagination to make things happen, strangely intermixes with divine power. On the one-dollar bill we read the words, "In God We Trust"; right next to those words, given equal prominence, we read, "Novus Ordo Seclorum"—the new secular order. The strong heroic implications of money make this particular mingling of divine and human intentions possible. Money in our possession enables us to imagine accomplishing something in the world; the lack of it seems to stop imagination short. Depending on the money in our possession, we can fulfill our fantasies—or not. Cash can turn fantasies into deeds, dreams into realities. The relationship between fantasy and its manifestation in reality is complex, in part because it is so indirect. Pure fantasy must go through filthy lucre in order to enter the world. I may want to become a lawyer. Or my favorite fantasy may be to drive down the street in a fire-red Porsche. Or I dream of educating children in exciting new ways. But all of these require financial backing if they are to come into human time.

From a psychological point of view, the old adage "Time is money," might better be reversed: "Money is time." Money brings fantasies out of the depths of the psyche and locates them in human time. Money provides the means for imagination to take root in the world. Psychologically, the *quantity* of money clearly does not stimulate the circulation of fantasy in the world. We can look around us, at wealthy people we've known or heard of, and see that simply having ready assets doesn't fulfill our fantasies at all. And when money is too quickly transformed into objects, there is little involvement with fantasy—no image to nurture, no way of coming to recognize our soul reflected in the *things* of the world.

In his book *Sacred Money*, Bernhard Laum states that our present sense of money recalls the city feasts of ancient Greece. These feasts were family celebrations, a coming together of all the families who made up the city. A great bull was often sacrificed for these gatherings, and if the feasts were very large, as many as fifty bulls were cooked, dismembered, and equally apportioned to each member of the clan. A portion, called the "surplus," was always left on the spit to be consumed by the fire, as an offering to the heroes of the past, who had become as gods.

As difficult as it may be for us who live in the modern world to grasp the full power of sacrificing the surplus to the heroes of the past, it is from this image that the action of money continues in our present world. The spit and the meat consumed by the ancestral fire is called the *obelos*, which we translate as "coin." *Obelos* has the same root as the word "obligation"—as we see it here, an obligation to the ancestors. As such, "surplus" is sacred, not something to be merely thrown away or used frivolously. The burnt offering unites the present with the past, the ancestral heroes with those living today.

A moneyed society represents more than a system of convenient barter. More than that, it incorporates the dead into the fabric of family and civil life. There is the underlying suggestion that the city exists not for the present alone but its future is less than tasteful without proper respect for the past. Such a society needs ways to publicly recognize its obligations to its ancestors in order to release the forces of imagination into financial matters. Portraits of its heroes, displayed in city buildings, public sculpture, fountains, and festivals, serve as daily reminders protecting the memorial value of our currency. These actions loosen the hold of quantitative economics and produce an economy of imagination.

Great cities and great nations perish because they can't join the beginning with the end, the past with the present. In their zealous drive for the new, they fail to see how they are pushed by the past, by the neglected older regime that has been driven from their memories. More and more, such a society becomes increasingly rigid, adhering to systems rather than caring for the imagination. It becomes management-centered instead of imagination-centered. Soon it no longer identifies itself as a living, sensuous body but as systems of economics, politics, and practical problems. If it is to awaken to its own imagination and creativity, the tightly bound, security-seeking organization of the city needs more loose change, coins musically jingling in the city treasury, gifts of the grandchildren delightfully honoring the ancestors.

Long ago, *obelos*, coin, was literally a meal ticket. A person who was not a family member could partake of the family feast by giving one of these coins. These meal tickets were often traded for goods, and they symbolized the surplus of the feast. The surplus, let's remember, the burnt offerings of the feast, connected the present with the past; those living in the present shared the feast, intermingling with their ancestors. It was believed that the ancients counseled those living in the present, giving advice, motivating actions of the family or community. The dead inspired the living, moved them to action. All of this was strongly felt in ancient times, and the coins themselves were literally tokens that gave whoever possessed them access to the ancestors' power. Removed from the rituals that paid homage to the past, the memory of our heroes dims, yet the power of the ancestors to affect action in the world does not.

The same meat that was eaten by the clan was sacrificed to the hero. Within the consciousness of those who took part in these feasts, there was the sense that the sacred surplus flowed into and was united with life-sustaining necessity. In the sacrifice, all that the hero represented was incorporated into the world of the living. This bodily communion gives human labors in the world a sacred character when we stop to reflect that food provides the energy for work; in addition, the food itself is energized by the ancestors. By feeding the spirit, the ancestors provide the support for shaping the world's body into the work of art that is the city. The ancestral heroes become visible, manifest in the qualities of city life; all the variety of life in the city—the impetus for the city to become a complete cosmos—memorializes the community of the dead.

The picture remains incomplete without an account of the bull, which nurtures present and past. The bull is virtually itself the imagination of new beginnings. James Hillman has traced the herd of mythological bulls throughout Western civilization—Taros, the bull rising from the sea; Istar's bull of the heaven, the bull Pasiphae; Dionysos as bull; the great bulls drawn on the ancient cave walls; the bull of the Mithraic religion; Psalm 22 in which Christ is slain by the bulls; the slaying of the bull by the great heroes; the American Indian imaging the world as a great bull. Wherever there are stories of beginnings, there are stories of bulls. (The word "capital" comes from "cattle," signifying the lump sum needed to initiate an action.)

The Nuer, an African tribe of South Sudan, still live by the bull. However, they do not sacrifice it. The anthropologist Evans Pritchard states:

> The men wake about dawn in the midst of their cattle and sit contentedly watching them till milking is finished. They then either take them to pasture and spend the day watching them graze, driving them to water, composing songs about them, and

bring them back to camp, or they remain in the kraal to drink their milk, make tethering cords and ornaments for them, eat and in other ways care for their calves, clean their kraal and dry their dung for fuel. Nuer wash their hands and face in the urine of cattle, especially when cows urinate during milking, drink their milk and blood, and sleep on their hides by the side of their smoldering dung. They cover their bodies, dress their hair and clear their teeth with ashes of cattle dung and eat their food with spoons made from their horns. When the cattle returned in the evening they tether each beast to its peg with cords made from the skins of their dead companions and sit in the wind screens to contemplate them and to watch them being milked.

For the Nuer, the bull is where the imagination of the world begins. But the Nuer do not have much of a civilization. There is no sacrifice of the bull, no apportionment of its meat and thus no movement of the imagination into multiple directions of actions. There is no guiding vision of the unity of action, inspired by the ancestors and branching out in a division of imagination that makes the city a complete world, a cosmos.

Money as a Standard of Wealth

IN SPITE OF THE FACT that paper money has not been backed by gold since 1934, gold has remained a permanent, archetypal image of the wealth represented by money. However, money is now backed by promises made by the government; there is more than a little faith in this backing. The word of the government, unfortunately, is not as good as gold. If words are to replace gold, they must be equally powerful; perhaps only poetry matches the golden backing of greenbacks.

Gold is rare. Gathered together, all the gold mined since the dawn of time would constitute about 80 thousand metric tons.

Piled in gold bricks, this would make a cube with sides 50 feet square, easily fitting within the lines of a baseball diamond. Gold is permanent, impervious to acids and corrosion. It endures; every ounce ever found still lies around somewhere. Gold is tremendously malleable; an ounce of gold, about the size of a half dollar, can be hammered into a thin sheet that would cover 100 square feet—a room ten feet by ten feet.

Gold is beautiful, capturing the essence of the sun itself; within our minds, it is as if gold connects us with the cosmos. Because of this connection, its permanent luster, its indestructibility, and its softness, more gold is made into art objects, jewelry, and ornaments than into bullion. The human hand making its mark in gold unites the human with the divine, for gold is a kind of immortality in a mortal world. What else could possibly account for the greed for gold, the raw passion it evokes, than the urge to have a touch of immortality?

Gold is also the earth under our feet. A final fantasy of gold is interesting because it is modern and counters the mythic fantasy of gold as the sun. In 1949, Dr. Harrison Brown of the University of Chicago, provided evidence that gold is plentiful at the core of the earth. He estimated that if it were possible to sink a hole 1500 meters in the earth, enough gold could be obtained to plate the surface of the entire earth several yards thick. Thus, the image of gold satisfies our highest aspirations and our deepest desires; it provides, in tangible form, a small glint, a touch of immortality—the final security each of us spends our life pursuing.

As long as money is backed by gold, money matters carry golden fantasies. Having money fuels the fantasy of being graced, gifted with the fortune of well-being. The circulation of gold coins provides us with the sense, on almost a daily basis, that gold permeates all things, gracing our daily lives with attributes of permanence, beauty, solidity, and fineness. When our money is backed by gold, all those golden qualities we have attributed to it, both mythic and real, are projected outward, to grace the city itself.

Clearly, when money is associated with gold, it has a powerful affect within our consciousnesses, and when it is dissociated from the gold, and all gold means to us, the things we buy with our money cease to have meaning. The poet Rilke expresses this well in his reflections on the pain associated with the disappearance of the golden age:

> To our grandparents, a "house," a "well," a "tower" familiar to them, even their own dress, their cloak, was infinitely more intimate; almost each thing a vessel in which they found something human and into which they set aside something human. Now, from America, empty indifferent things, dummies of life, are crowding over to us . . . a house in the American understanding, an American apple or a grapevine there, has nothing in common with the house, the fruit, the grapes into which went the hopes and meditations of our forefathers.

In 1908, before the gold standard was abandoned, and before Rilke put into public discourse the decline of a truly human economy, Freud had already discovered what had happened to the standard of wealth. Within the society of his time, and for a variety of complex reasons, it had shifted from the highest values of immortal splendor to the lowliest of the low; in the minds of many it had, in a word, turned to shit. Quite straightforwardly, Freud stated: "money is feces."

In the beginning, many people dismissed this statement as absurd. But Freud was actually getting at some very important qualities that had come to be associated with money. He saw that behind expressions such as "dirty money," "filthy lucre," "the smell of cash," "putting someone on a retainer," "tight money," "loose money," and cash "flow" were shadows of our true feelings about money. He suggested that within the subconscious, from which the shadow is projected, money had come to have a dirty side.

We can argue this point perhaps, but it is difficult to refute the fact that if we follow them far enough many activities involving money take us right into the "messes" of the world. Money's shadow, indeed, has a dark side when we realize that great power struggles are focused on money, laws are broken to get it, confidences are violated, families divided, and murders committed in its name.

We have to understand Freud's concerns with the anal character to explore in any depth his perception of money, and the "dirty" side of our associations with it. It is primarily through the anal character that money becomes associated with feces and we begin applying values to it that would ordinarily apply only to our bodily functions. The anal character traits, of course, permeated 19th- and early 20th-century culture, particularly in Europe, spreading throughout most of the Western world. We must assume that these traits became part of our associations with money and with the shadow it casts.

Freud observed that the anal retentive person obsesses about control, holds onto, accumulates, and hoards money as if holding onto it had value in itself—which, of course, is no more true of money than it is of feces! It was his point that this retentive behavior, applied to money, had become a major force in our society. In this climate, activities involving money become tightly held secrets, to be conducted only in strict privacy, behind closed doors. Out of this secrecy comes a kind of paranoia where money is concerned, based on a distortion about the meaning of money—mainly that it must be accumulated and hoarded, and that there was something inherently "dirty" about it.

Freud's real contribution can be found in his making a reconnection between money matters and the functions of the body, the sense that the health of both the individual and communal body depends on movement and energy for both money and feces. The introduction of his metaphor into our lives seems a healthy sign. It brings home to us the fact that money has no value in and of itself, making us become more aware that money is a waste unless it is tended, cultivated, and given the care of the imagination.

The child psychologist Jean Piaget observed that children sometimes experience excrement as alive. One child told him: "You know the noise my tummy makes? Well, it's all my plops squeaking. They speak if they're hungry." When Piaget asked if the plops were alive, the child answered, "Oh, yes. They're alive because they're inside me. But they die as soon as they come out. That's why they like to stay inside."

Freud, of course, was not the first one to reflect on the associations people have made between shit, money, gold, and immortality. In ancient Egypt, for example, the scarab beetle was venerated because it seemed to have the capacity to reproduce itself by rolling up in a ball of dung. A single, rolled-up beetle would, in a short period of time, and with the help of shit, become several beetles. It seemed capable of self-regeneration and immortality without the need for a mother.

Within the human psyche, both gold and shit appear as having life-generating capacities. But there are certain interesting distinctions made between the two. The archetypal image of gold suggests a divine element—the gift of immortality, a connection with the eternal. It gives lofty, regal inspiration to the human world. It motivates, sparks the imagination, contributing to the making of the cosmos. Shit, meanwhile, suggests that creation depends on the human will, just as toilet training concerns the will to hold on and let go, to save and spend.

Is it any wonder that we are so ambivalent about money? The power of its shadow is rich, complex, and challenging. It is divine and filthy; it promises immortality on one hand, death on the other; it is priceless, and it is worthless. Within our consciousnesses it appears filled with contradiction—paradoxes that seem to have no easy resolution, keeping us always a little off balance.

For the infant, there is deep satisfaction in the act of defecation. It is one of our first experiences of self-expression. We are literally creating something out of our own bodies. Somehow, the image of "sitting on the throne," calling up as many references to defecation as to royalty, seems apropos.

Throughout folk literature and the oral storytelling tradition of ancient peoples, there have been powerful psychological parallels between defecation and giving birth within the human psyche, almost since the beginning of time. While creativity, defecation, and gold appears to be universally mingled in our consciousness of money, the association between defecation and birth appears to be predominantly a male fantasy. Perhaps it is "womb envy," the male counterpart of "penis envy" which Freud attributed to women. And if we press this image to its logical conclusion, we see that within the shadow may also be found the man's obsession with making money as an effort to compensate for the lack of a womb.

There's an interesting example of this intermingling between man's labors, feces, and giving birth in an ancient story from the Siberian Eskimo culture. It is told that Big Raven takes his sledge to the woods to peel the alder bark.

After a while, he has to defecate. When he does, he excretes one large, thick piece of shit. He looks at it lying in the snow and says, "There! I have given birth to a pretty woman. I will marry her." The rest of the story has to do with the disasters that ensue when he brings Excrement Woman home and, blind in his arrogance, tries to impose her upon his household.

Similarly, the renowned folklorist Geshon Legman tells of a man who wanted to know how a woman feels when she becomes a mother, a story drawn from the early American tradition. To show him, the doctor plugs the man's anus, feeds him a quart of castor oil, and puts him to bed. The man has increasingly agonizing cramps and spasms, from which he is distracted only by the sound of an organ grinder out in the street. The organ grinder's monkey climbs in the window and perches on the edge of the bed just as the stopper pops out of the man's anus. Shit explodes all over the monkey. The man lies there dazed for a moment, then hears the squeal of the little beast. He raises his head in delight, hugs the monkey to his bosom, and cries, "You're ugly, you're hairy, you're all covered in shit but you are mine and I love you."

Money and Retention

THE CHILD IN PIAGET'S STORY saw feces as valuable and alive only when it was retained within the body. When separated from the body, it died, lost all value. Perhaps this same mechanism is the psychological basis for modern economics, focusing on the pleasure and power of accumulating, retaining, and releasing money (feces) at will. We can turn to the legendary Howard Hughes as the archetypal hero of this model. Never does he yield to the feminine, to those values associated with releasing and nurturing what we have created. Hughes had no children that he would admit to, though there have been many who claimed he was their father. And he was so detached from the feminine that he was able to exploit feminine beauty for the sake of making and accumulating more money. During his adventure into movie-making, he introduced sex into the modern film with the famous scene of the bosomy Jane Russell lounging sensuously in the hay.

His biographers tell us that Hughes was as tight with his own excrement as he was with his money, suffering from chronic constipation during his entire adult life. He developed an extreme phobia of germs. He would not eat from silverware, and those attending him were required to wear surgical gloves. He would not touch anything except with a tissue in his hand to protect him. He would allow neither his hair nor his fingernails to be cut, obsessively retaining all that his body produced. It is perhaps fitting that he did not die close to the earth but in an airplane. And his money, bequeathed to no one, remains in his name even in death.

It is easy to make an association between retention of money and the banking industry. Banks retain money. They develop tight, complex systems of control to account for every bit of it—what comes in, what is retained, what is allowed to go out, as well as the "interest" which accumulates when it is retained or loaned to another person.

Shit is also fertilizer. Like the manure spread on the ground to stimulate the growth of the farmer's crops, money as cash, money easily transferred, invested as capital to start new ventures, stimulates economic growth. The association with feces is reflected in both tight and loose money. Once it is no longer backed by the gold standard, and by all our psychological associations with gold or other precious minerals, the value of money is governed by the rhythms of retention and expression, controlled by the "sphincter" of the state.

Money as feces brings financial matters into the world of the body and the senses. In this respect, we are reminded that without the body there can be no shadow; we literally and figuratively hold the shadow within our bodies. Since feces is more universal than gold (everyone makes it!), the money as feces metaphor spreads the image of wealth more equally around the world. When money rests under the sign of excrement, Everyman sits on his own throne. Royalty is shared by all. The city is then built not just by those sitting on the highest throne but also by those grunting on the lowest seats. The highest aspirations of God and our ancestral heroes share the space with a spread of commodities for the common man—even if these commodities do begin to stink and melt away like Big Raven's Excrement Woman. When it comes to money, gold and feces need one another, just as the shadow needs the body as well as the light.

The Alchemy of Gold into Plastic

IT IS INTERESTING TO NOTE that it was a work of fiction, not the creative brainstorm of an economist, that gave us the credit card. In 1887, a lawyer and journalist by the name of Edward Bellamy wrote a utopian novel entitled *Looking Backward*. In that work, he described an idea intended to free the world from money in the 20th century:

> A credit corresponding to his share of the annual product of the nation is given to every citizen on the public books at the beginning of each year, and a credit issued him with which he procures

at the public storehouse, found in every community, whatever he desires whenever he desires it. This arrangement, you will see, totally obviates the necessity for business transactions of any sort between individuals and consumers.

Credit cards take money, with all its shadow associations, out of circulation, removing it from the vitality of the communal body. They eliminate memory and withdraw the body from the work of the imagination. Founded on a utopian ideal, a world without place, without human action, credit cards fool us into believing that acquisition is limited only by the imagination. As a Montgomery Ward president once said: "A regular charge customer buys two and a half to three times more in a year than an average cash customer . . . I'd estimate that sales of appliances, furniture, tires, and other expensive items would drop 35 to 40 percent if credit were suddenly disconnected."

Credit consumerism makes it possible to fantasize that desires can be fulfilled without the usual impediments of human commerce. In order for this persuasion to succeed, however, the imagistic value of money must be forgotten, discarded. Memory, purpose, and body all yield to pure fancy; nothing stands between the credit card and the things we want. But the less value we find in money itself, in the feel of gold coin in our palms, or in the pictures of our ancestral heroes in our wallets, connecting us with the earth, bodily functions, and the past, the more we look to the objects we buy, expecting them to give our lives and our imaginations substance. The less real, the more "plastic" our system of exchange becomes, the more we become disconnected from the body and human community.

Money concerns us all as a standard of wealth. We have yet to learn that true wealth can only be measured in the quality of life. It is to this well-being that money needs to be directed—not simply seen as a way to purchase goods. To get to this point of understanding, we need to instill money with the merit of memory, the wealth inherent in craft, and to achieve that end we must begin to see it in its capacity to mediate, to establish a medium of exchange between one provider of goods or services and another.

Money as a Medium of Exchange

MONEY IS NOT A THING. It represents an action, to be considered as a verb and adverb rather than a noun. It is more like the action of imagination's energy—divine, as we saw in the stories of sacrifice in ancient time, or in our exploration of money and feces. It can be useful to think of money as the ever-present interactions of two wills—the poetic tension that joins two imaginations in a medium of exchange. It is almost as if the act of "moneying" the world is an erotic transaction, freeing the imagination to circulate widely in the material world and then materializing into visible forms. Or, if you prefer, it is the alchemical catalyst that transforms imagination into actions and physical objects.

Imagine giving twenty-five cents for an apple. I used the verb "giving" rather than "spending" to alert us to the ritual quality of the interaction, which departs from the economics of possessiveness. To think of this act as spending places the whole operation into the logic of cause and effect, while the act of giving, done so automatically through the body, implies that there is a complex relation of patterns going on. The magic and charm flee from the action when both coin and fruit are fixed as material qualities divorced from the human activities represented in the exchange. Giving twenty-five cents is the release of imagined desire into the world. It allows us to transform our imagined desire for the apple into the actuality of the apple.

To begin relating to money as a mediator, we have to slow down enough to give attention to what is actually happening. We have to begin seeing how money is part of a whole complex of ongoing relationships—with family, employers, store keepers, city, and world. The whole point of budgeting money into the major categories of life is to keep us emotionally in touch with as many of these relationships as possible. However, budgets need not be seen as static entries on an accountant's form; rather, they are momentary accounts of what our imagination does in relation to the world, an acknowledgment of the actual value of moment. The moment of exchange becomes a ritual moment, compactly rendering the significance of individual and communal imaginations.

In *The Odyssey* there is a wonderful description of a sacrificial feast like the one we explored at the beginning of this essay. There are nine long tables, spread out for the people of Pylos; at each of them there are seated 500 citizens, each group with nine bulls sacrificed in honor of the gods. The banqueters are clothed in white robes, and each one wears a crown. The feast begins with prayers and libations. Hymns are sung. The nature of the dishes and the kinds of wine being served are regulated by the laws of the city. To deviate in the least—to present a new dish or alter the rhythms of the hymns—was considered a grave impiety. This strict attention to detail and procedure shows the importance of a particular discipline in any work of imagination. Our own relationship with money requires a similar kind of discipline and attention.

Like the sacrificial feast, money is a specialized ritual, making visible the gift of the community and the need or desire of the individual. In the process of mediating the transactions between them, money supports the making of a culture. From this vantage point, wealth does not depend on cash accumulated—which itself can never be the measure of well-being, as we have clearly seen in the case of Howard Hughes. A real sense of worth cannot be experienced except with a sensitive, aesthetic awareness of the qualities of the ritual transaction. A quarter for an apple can be worth a great deal or very little. It all depends on the comprehensiveness of the feelings involved in the exchange. Money can be an expression of our love for the world when we begin to put our transactions in the form of gifts. When we experience such transactions as a reaching back in gratitude to our ancestors, outward to embrace a network of communal ties, and inward to embrace resources for the soul, then we are living in a city that recognizes our true worth.

Money is a kind of magic talisman, through which transformations of the city take place. When we relate to money only as a quantity, we enter the economics of fear and power. Those with the greatest accumulated quantities protect their interests and as a result the city develops in lopsided ways, like a body with a tumor. When the mass gets too ugly to ignore any longer, beauticians are brought in to do a facial. By contrast, when we imagine money from a qualitative vantage point, we enter the economics of delight.

In the modern world it is easy to fall into the habit of thinking that the things we buy will bring pleasure in and of themselves. What we too easily forget is that pleasure is found not in things acquired but in the gathering of friends to share in the flow of the wealth.

Money is a perfect medium, a flexible metaphor that can operate in a variety of ways. A dollar bill can become a pack of cigarettes, a phone call to a friend, a half-gallon or so of gasoline, or a hamburger at a fast-food restaurant. The economics of accumulation and possessiveness ruins the metaphor, replacing it with a sanitized and simplistic cause-effect structure, controlled by an accountant who is dedicated only to a system of checks and balances. Money as ritual is a very different thing.

The word "ritual" comes from the Latin *ritus*, from the Greek *hroe*, meaning "to flow, run, rush, or stream." Ritual literally places you in the flow of things. The flow of cash moves imagination into the world. In turn, the needs of the imagination shape the world. When viewed in this way, the language of money takes on very different and vital meanings. "Saving" is no longer just accumulation and hoarding but the intensification of value. "Investing" becomes a way to lay claim on imagination, drawing it closer and paying closer attention to how it functions and how we might better use it in the world. "Profit" is an intriguing concept here since it easily makes us forget the ritual quality of money, placing the value on accumulation and money for its own sake. We think of ancient adages such as, "What does a *profit* a man to gain the whole world and lose his soul?" Profit is not intended to be accumulated but to be further *invested* in the imagination.

I said that money is more like a verb than a noun. It worries us whenever we try to circumscribe it or pin it down. Note that while we can pin down a noun in this way, the action of a verb constantly slips away, eluding us. Money problems are so difficult to bring under control because they signify a whole dynamic complex of interactions gone awry. When such problems occur, the primary financial consultant must be our own soul. We must dip back in time to the archetypal ritual feast where the actions of daily life become sacred, with each act involving money related to a greater totality, a holistic community whose actions and imagination form the woof and warp of an infinite tapestry.

We are so accustomed to viewing money as a noun, a static object that we exchange for another static object that we find it difficult to sense the ritual flow we are involved in. We believe that the thing we want to buy will bring us pleasure, fill a need, and that's as far as we can take it. We have become so separated from the ritual flow that we no longer see that the pleasure comes from our experiencing that flow for itself.

When we violate the flow by trying to control it, when we attempt to divert its action for our own selfish purposes and personal gain, totally ignoring the larger picture in which we're involved, we become like the man who lives upriver and builds a dam to divert all the water to his own fields, literally creating a drought in the valley below the dam. It is a sin, a violation against the essential nature of money. The result is a money neurosis—guilt-ridden spending or hoarding. Every time I feel bad I spend money and momentarily feel good again. Soon afterwards I feel guilty again and start the whole cycle all over again, controlling, hanging on, instead of letting go.

Freud says, I think quite accurately, that obsessive ritualism is an expression of repressed sexuality. When we experience guilt because we have violated the flow of money, we have repressed not sexuality per se, so much as the sensual body experiences of participating fully in the flow.

On Mothers, Miserly Sons, and Money— A Concluding Image

IN THE *LOUISVILLE COURIER*, on August 16, 1961, an article appeared, telling of a man found dead in his apartment, among trash accumulated over half a century. In the five-room flat, police found nearly $47,000 in cash, much of it tucked among articles such as old newspapers and magazines, phonograph records, thousands of packs of safety matches, dozens of wedding bands and diamond rings, a carton of more than a hundred harmonicas, a zither, a birdcage, razors and razor blades. Some rooms were five feet deep in the hoards of similar articles, and by the time the police had finished going through the material, they had found more than eighty bank books, with total deposits of over $112,000. Many of them had only ten dollar deposits, the records of accounts the man had opened for the premiums, such as toasters and electric coffee pots, that banks offered new account holders.

This particular miser had come from a wealthy family: his father had made millions in real estate; his brothers had been bankers. While his mother lived she clung to her sons, administering to their needs as if they were children.

Like the Howard Hughes story, this one echoes a theme of money gone awry in a person's life. Stories such as this are less common than they were even fifty years ago. But the same underlying theme has not disappeared by any means. The miser of yesterday is today's consumer. Both are caught up in the fantasy that the true value of money is in the money itself or in the objects it can buy. Memories are hoarded; wealth is hoarded; money itself is hoarded. The modern consumer, like the miser, tries to dam up the flow, divert, and hold onto whatever he can. He values *possession* above all else, blind to the ritual nature of money.

When all one's energies are aimed at holding onto one's wealth, junk piles up around us. The basements and garages of middle-class homes all over the country are filled with evidence of this modern-day hoarding. Consumer goods, some items used only once or twice, are stacked to the rafters. It all sits there, like formless lumps, slowly rotting away, to one day be hauled off to the overflowing dumps, to return to the earth who gives birth to everything and claims it back.

While the resources of Mother Earth last, the wasteful drama of the consumer-hoarder goes unnoticed, as does the underlying theme of disconnection and fear that fosters it. As long as the inheritance of the father is retained, there is a sense of security. But when the mother dies, the miser emerges. Then comes the fear of not having. The miser fears, cannot imagine having to go into debt. The fear of debt is the fear of having no future. Both the miser and the consumer are fraught with insecurities of this kind, driven by a fear that can never be remedied by the route he has taken to comfort himself.

There is one last observation about the miser in our story above. The household was completely lacking in the kind of order that is apparent when the imagination is alive and well. Cash, diamond rings, and expensive objects were tossed among junk such as old newspapers and trash, revealing that the hoarding itself took precedence over all else. The hoarding impulse was so dominant that it had literally killed the imagination.

As we look more closely at the acts of misers, we begin to more clearly see the hidden characters of money. When possession itself becomes the main purpose of money, we become blind to the future. And money without a future is a world falling apart, a world in disarray, as symbolized by the miser's apartment. By contrast, when money acts, increasing rather than damming up the flow of energy through our lives, it stimulates change. I do not mean change in the manner we usually mean it when we speak of "progress," for progress as we know it in the modern world, is but another form of control, of exploiting the resources of Mother Earth. Rather, I am speaking of the change that comes about in our relationships with each other, our past, and the building of the city that we saw in our early discussions concerning the great feasts and the founding of the city.

Mere quantity can never replace quality if we are to build vital cities such as our ancient forefathers enjoyed. To begin doing that, we must abandon the economics we have known since the 19th century. At that time, there was a strange marriage between physical science, the science of numbers, and money. We were convinced that the way to a better world was through the *quantification* of human behavior around money matters. Control became the byword and money became viewed as a measurable quantity, its value measured only by its own actual value or the value of the hard goods it could buy.

To revive the vital role of money in our lives, we must begin to look upon it as imagination's way of acting in the world. We must begin seeing it as the making of a worldly imagination.

PART VII

Prejudice

Introduction

Hate has a lot in common with love,
chiefly with that self-transcending aspect of love,
the fixation on others, the dependence on them
and in fact the delegation of a piece of one's own
identity to them . . .
the hater longs for the object of his hatred.

—Vaclav Havel

I have a dream today.
With this faith we will
be able to transform
the tangled discord of our nation
into a beautiful symphony of brotherhood.
I have a dream that one day
this nation will rise up
and live out the true meaning of its creed:
"We hold these truths to be self-evident;
that all men are created equal."

—Martin Luther King, Jr., 1963

MOST AMERICANS ARE PROUD OF THEIR NATION'S HERITAGE. The United States has been a beacon of freedom to the world, illuminating hope for oppressed peoples everywhere. We are the melting pot culture, the land of opportunity, a refuge, as promised on the Statue of Liberty:

Give me your tired, your poor,
Your huddled masses yearning to breathe free,
The wretched refuse of your teeming shore.
Send these, the homeless, tempest-tost to me,
I lift my lamp beside the golden door!

This is a colossal promise, not one about which any of us can be cynical. Except for Native Americans, everyone here comes from immigrant stock. For over 200 years we have symbolized the promise of a better future, a time when all peoples on earth can live side-by-side in peace and harmony, "with liberty and justice for all." Though that time may seem far away today, the ideals behind this promise are not hollow. They are palpable facts of reality. A culture needs ideals and vision, and the American vision is broad and inclusive. People have been willing to die to support these notions because they deliver, and we are the beneficiaries of their worthiness.

But, hold the flags and patriotic huzzahs for a moment . . . our national pride may augur our national shame. The loftier the ideal, the deeper the plunge. Rather than take the posture of a sentimental patriot or of a skeptical detractor, we must find a balance in our idealism. The one-sided get blind-sided.

Very few among us would admit to racial prejudice. What we would most vehemently deny about our shortcomings is perhaps what we need most to examine. As a nation, we are disgraced daily by the face of racial bigotry and ethnic prejudice, by hate crimes and quotas, red-lining and ghettoizing, name-calling and cross-burning. This problem belongs to all of us.

What are the mechanisms at work in the human psyche that cause us to fail to live up to our ideals? We suffer from a great cultural disease that is common to all human societies:

Prejuduce divides our hearts and our minds into love and hate, us and them. Our hypocrisy cries out to be challenged, to be understood.

In "The Scapegoat Archetype," Sylvia Brinton Perera offers us an explanation of the complex psychology underlying our prejudiced attitudes and behavior. Her work is objective, claiming no easy resolution of the scapegoating problem.

Jerome S. Bernstein's essay, "An Archetypal Dilemma: The LA Riots," utilizes the psychological tools that Ms. Perera has developed in her piece. He describes and analyzes the prevailing conditions experienced by our largest minority (12 percent), African Americans. His view of the contemporary events following the Rodney King beating dramatically illustrates how the neglect of our collective racist shadow, which historically has been projected onto Blacks, resulted in these tragic consequences. Taken together, these two authors provide both the theory and application for a shadow inquiry into prejudice.

—J. A.

– The Scapegoat Archetype –

SYLVIA BRINTON PERERA

If only it were all so simple! If only there were evil
   people
somewhere insidiously committing evil deeds, and it
   were
necessary only to separate them from the rest of us and
   destroy
them. But the line dividing good and evil cuts through
   the
heart of every human being. And who is willing to
   destroy a
piece of his own heart?
   —Alexander Solzhenitsyn, *The Gulag Archipelago*

TODAY WE USE THE TERM "SCAPEGOAT" easily in discussion of collective morality. We have become attuned to finding the phenomenon of scapegoating in social psychology, and there are many studies of the scapegoat pattern in small groups, in families, in ethnic and national politics.

We apply the term to individuals and groups who are accused of causing misfortune. This serves to relieve others, the scapegoaters, of their own responsibilities, and to strengthen the scapegoaters' sense of power and righteousness. In this current usage a search for the scapegoat relieves us also of our relationship to the transpersonal dimension of life, for in the present age we have come to function with a perverted form of the archetype, one that ignores the gods, and we blame the scapegoat and the devil for life's evils.

We forget that originally the scapegoat was a human or an animal victim chosen for sacrifice to the underworld god to propitiate that god's anger and to heal the community. The scapegoat was a *pharmakon* or healing agent. In the scapegoat rituals it was dedicated to and identified with the god. It functioned to bring the transpersonal dimension to aid and renew the community, for the community acknowledged that it was embedded in and dependent on transpersonal forces. The scapegoat ritual, like others, was used "to enrich meaning or call attention to other levels of existence. . . . [It] incorporate[d] evil and death along with life and goodness into a single, grand, unifying pattern."[1]

Today we still believe in the efficacy of a magic ritual action. But we are too often unconscious of the "grand, unifying pattern," the transpersonal matrix in which our actions are embedded. We see only the material, secular framework of the actions and ignore the spiritual dimension to which they were originally intended to connect us. Thus a modern psychologist writes:

> [There is] a general Western belief that catastrophe can be averted by the appropriate prophylactic action, whether it be baptism or breast feeding. We would like to believe in a prescription . . . that can innoculate . . . against future misery and failure.[2]

This desire to avert catastrophe is worldwide and forms the basis of religious and magic ritual. In the modern age, however the scapegoat ritual has gone bad because it has become trivialized. Its deeper meaning is unconscious. We tend to feel that mankind and/or the devil bring evil into the world, since God is only good. But this means that mankind is also felt to be nearly omnipotent, capable of averting evil without recourse to those forces of destiny far greater than human will.

Scapegoating, as it is currently practiced, means finding the one or ones who can be identified with evil or wrong-doing, blamed for it, and cast out from the community in order to leave the remaining members with a feeling of guiltlessness, atoned (at-one) with the collective standards of behavior. It both allocates blame and serves to "innoculate against future misery and failure" by evicting the presumed cause of misfortune. It gives the illusion that we can be "perfect,"[3] if we take the proper prophylactic measures, do the right things.

In Jungian terms, scapegoating is a form of denying the shadow of both man and God. What is seen as unfit to conform with the ego ideal, or with the perfect goodness of God, is repressed and denied, or split off and made unconscious. It is called devilish. We do not consciously confess our faults and wayward impulses over the scapegoat's head in order to atone with the spiritual dimensions as did the ancient Hebrews. We do not often enough even see that they are part of our psychological makeup. But we are acutely aware of their belonging to others, the scapegoats. We see the shadow clearly in projection. And the scapegoater feels a relief in being lighter, without the burden of carrying what is unacceptable to his or her ego ideal, without shadow. Those who are identified with the scapegoat, on the other hand, are identified with the unacceptable shadow qualities. They feel inferior, rejected, and guilty. They feel responsible for more than their personal share of shadow. But both scapegoater and scapegoat feel in control of the mix of goodness and malevolence that belongs to reality itself.

The medieval and modern perversion of the archetype have produced a pathology that is widespread. There are many scapegoats among us, individuals identified with the archetype and caught in the distorted pattern in which it now operates. In the following pages I will explore some of the ramifications of the scapegoat archetype as it applies to the clinical phenomenology of scapegoat-identified individuals. The image of the scapegoat provides vectors of comprehension that illuminate what is behind a common dis-ease felt by many of us. Thus, in C. G. Jung's words, it permits "consciousness . . . [to be] born of unconsciousness ."[4] Following the layers of the complex in its current pathological form down into the structures of the original archetypal image provides clues for the healing of the individuals caught in the scapegoat complex.

Readers will need to proceed slowly and to remember that, although the material here is necessarily presented in linear form, its focus is on the total gestalt—the immediate and whole structure of the archetypal image. The many factors described exist simultaneously in the timeless and dense pattern of the image itself.

My understanding is derived from my own experience of the complex, from material shared by friends and from clinical work with analysands. The scapegoat complex is widespread. To some extent we all share its salient features, although these are most clearly seen in certain cases. The difference is one of degree of identification with the archetype and hence weakness of ego. The structure of the complex remains the same.

The Meaning of the Scapegoat Archetype

THE SCAPEGOAT PHENOMENON is a particular expression, along with Cain, Ishmael, Satan, witch-hunting, minority persecution, and war, of the general problem of shadow projection. It is, as we know from anthropological data, an almost universal phenomenon. In cultures where conscious connection to the transpersonal source has not been lost, the one identified with the scapegoat serves the community by returning evil to its archetypal source through sacrifice, carrying back to the gods a burden too great for the human collective to bear. In Western culture, those who suffer identification with the archetype share the burden of the central divinity of our eon, for the archetype of the Messiah as Suffering Servant is at the core of the Western psyche. We all feel its power and share its effects to some extent.

When in the modern age individuals are deeply identified with the role of the scapegoat, they suffer the symptoms discussed above—they endure negative inflation, exile, and splitting. They are cut off from an adequate relation to the outer world and to their own inner depths. But even after they are able to disidentify from the burden of the complex, they have a special relation to the archetype. "The complex becomes a focus of life," [5] for their personalities have been built within its pattern. Thus they are "called" to carry the complex consciously. These individuals are left with a need to discover and relate consciously to its specific meaning in their lives. In this search and service is their healing.

Such service implies a conscious relation to one's own wounds, those places of shame wherein the scapegoat-identified individual felt the pain of being a pariah, cut off from the Self still projected onto the parental container. Initially, these wounds turned into the scar tissue that perpetuated the loss of relations to the external collective and the transpersonal through unconscious splitting. Through conscious sacrifice of the inflated, collective identity as scapegoat and savior, these wounds can better be borne openly— suffered as open conflicts between the voice of the collective and the messages of the individual Self. Just as the spear wound in Christ's side was seen to be the womb of the Church, so these wounds can be seen as the vessel of one's own individual soul, bringing forth the individual as one is destined to be. One's vulnerability is seen then as a service to life.

This restored sense of wholeness permits leaving the collective to go forth consciously and with conscience, bearing some measure of one's own shadow. Jung has stressed that struggling with one's own shadow permits a degree of self-reliance and psychological autonomy, an enlargement of consciousness, the sacrifice of the ideal of perfection for one of wholeness, and some relativization of good and evil—clearly necessary if we are all to live on one planet. Erich Neumann further suggests that bearing one's own shadow liberates the collective:

> In contrast to scapegoat psychology, in which the individual eliminates his own evil by projecting it on to the weaker brethren, we now find that the exact opposite is happening: we encounter the phenomenon of "vicarious suffering." The individual assumes personal responsibility for part of the burden on the collective, and he decontaminates this evil by integrating it into his own inner process of transformation. If the operation is successful, it leads to an inner liberation of the collective, which in part at least is redeemed from this evil.[6]

One young woman brought a dream which imaged her as one who relieved the collective of its shadow material. She had been in therapy for five years and had just returned from a visit to her sanctimonious parental home, depressed and regressively identified with her victimized ego. She dreamt:

> I am walking through my parents' house. It's also like my grandparents' house. It's a mess. I seem to have a pile of their old

garbage that I have to carry out. I find a pit outside the back door. It's a large, lead-lined hole in the ground.

She associated the garbage to the anger she had felt when her minister father had humiliated her children and dominated their activities in order to enhance his persona before his parishioners. She had expressed her feelings, but she had not felt them understood. She knew consciously that she felt her children's treatment so poignantly because it reminded her of countless experiences of her own with her father. She was aware of his human limitations and even of what she called his "pious-preacher's dissociation." She knew she had been the family scapegoat and felt the family power-shadow keenly. Now this dream brought the new realization that her rage was not hers alone, but part of the ancestral shadow that she had been handed to deal with.

Because the garbage pit had a lead lining, she thought the waste material must be radioactive. She mused:

It can't be put safely into the air, the water, or the earth. All that ministerial power stuff, that rage. It's too potent. What is that lead-lined container for me?

We had talked about her own old schizoid defenses as an inert, unfeeling containment. She originally imaged them as a "leaden facade." The garbage pit was a variation on the theme, but it was open and already grounded. She decided it referred to the psychodramatic and ritualized enactments of her rage that she had performed earlier in her analysis. Spontaneously she picked up a piece of driftwood in the office and, using it like a dagger, she began to move. With increasing fury she danced. When she was done she glowed—her own life energy had returned. She explained she had done the dance of Jael, the Kenite heroine in the Old Testament. By connecting to an archetypal image of murderousness and expressing its dark affect, she was able to carry forward the dream and contain the collective shadow impulse within a ritual and aesthetic form.

Further reflection on the image of Jael showed us that it was a particularly apt one. It mirrored precisely the woman's experience of the ancestral dissociation, but in a redeemed and conscious form. Jael lured the enemy general Sisera with milk and offers of protection in order to murder him. Yet she is honored; in the Song of Deborah she is called "blessed . . . among women . . . among all women that dwell in tents may she be blessed."[7] The patient's parents covered their psychologically murderous power urge with a veneer of pious goodness and hospitality. The woman herself had identified with the innocent persona; and, split off from her aggressiveness, she had also identified herself as a victim. The active imagination in ritual dance reintegrated the shadow energies by making them conscious, containing both persona and shadow within a strong, feminine Self image, one which could carry the ancestral garbage.

Such a conscious suffering of the collective power shadow not only somewhat liberated those in her immediate environment, but also gradually made this woman "psychologically noninfectious."[8] She became increasingly able to confront her parents and others without becoming infected by their anger. She also became able to deal in her relationships with conscious, adaptive assertiveness instead of poisoning contagious resentment.

Just as the priest of the Yoruba smallpox cult, who alone treats patients with the disease, is himself recovered from the disease and therefore immune, so the individual disidentified from the scapegoat complex can confront similar wounds and

guilt in others and become an agent of consciousness and healing. The dream of one man who went on to become an analyst
illustrates how the process of disidentification served to permit
his becoming a healer. He dreamt:

> I am in France where I find a medieval city that is now modern-
> ized, the old churches surrounded by modern houses. There are
> many individual styles among the architecture. There is also a
> display of the only type of architecture not permitted—a win-
> dowless arched cave, which has a bloated, big-headed dummy
> male figure in it, like a diver who lives off piped supplies. I show
> the friend I am with, and we agree that is a horrible way to live. I
> meet my woman friend. She has finished medical school. We
> decide to leave the town to go into the desert. She doesn't want to
> come until I persuade her we can write a new *materia medica* for
> desert life. She accepts because that is a sufficient life challenge.

This man associated a beloved aunt and his conversations
with her, with France, one of the few early places his feelings
ever flowed. The medieval walled city (the complex, a
defended place of clear-cut collective virtue and vice) has been
modernized: each individual is given the possibility of a
uniquely designed psychic space within the whole. The diverse
aspects of the dreamer have space and are accepted. Only the
old encapsulating schizoid defensiveness is forbidden. The
dreamer felt the cave to be an image of his old fear of loneliness. It was the primary symptom of his scapegoat complex. To
the dummy he associated his mindless accommodating posture
that needed "piped supplies" because he couldn't relate
humanly and directly. But more positively, the dummy also
suggested the idea of being a "psychological diver," an
explorer of the unconscious.

In the lysis of the dream, accepting the loneliness consciously becomes the cure: The dreamer and his healer-anima sacrifice the collective life and willingly go into the wilderness to discover a new healing repertoire. Consciously consenting to the individuation potential within the archetype becomes a life's work; the pathology suffered through and borne consciously becomes a calling to serve—not in the old collectively appeasing ways, but as a wounded-healer who dares to venture beyond the collective walls to where the Self calls. As this man finally reconciled to his fate put it:

> My parents sent me away so I could learn the feeling way that they could never teach me. But now in their old age they need it and so do many others. They seek me out. I feel like the Prodigal Son. It almost makes the exile years seem a destined misery that I could grow from.

The wilderness, here entered consciously, expresses the scapegoat's true relation to the gods. Through alienation from the collective, the scapegoat serves in a medial capacity, helping to connect the world of consciousness to that of the objective psyche. Such service to the transpersonal requires an heroic and conscious venturing into the otherworld, places considered evil, archaic, terrible—those very wilderness regions that were originally the scapegoat-identified individual's personal hell, but where now the numinous energies can be met with the new attitudes born through the transformation process.

The scapegoat is one of many images that suggest the interface between consciousness and unconsciousness. Along with artists, priests, shamans, clowns, and witches, the scapegoat crosses the boundary of the collective and deals with material too fraught with danger and chaos for ordinary secular hands. Along with these others the scapegoat serves to redeem the old modalities, specifically by having to confront and struggle with the material repressed by the culture.

The "be ye perfect" demands of our own inner demonic accuser—the one-sided supercritical judge of our actions—loses its distorted and esoteric meaning as an imperative to live up to collective behavioral standards. It becomes instead an invitation to the service of the spirit as it manifests individually to a deeply attuned consciousness. It becomes a call to discover this inherent mode of knowledge—initially by the very task of "working through" the scapegoat complex itself. It becomes a call to discover the destiny which granted this painful role as an awakener of the redeeming spirit within.

Here psychotherapy takes its rightful place as a stepping-stone toward the knowledge of the individual's true essence—the Self—and the meaning of one's current fate on earth.

A remarkable dream of another woman, who was working her way out of the complex, presents an image of the profound process by which she was taught about the transpersonal source of good and evil:

My father is a drunk. I am running young slaves across the border, hiding them on the decks of slow boats that are moving north. I take them to homes where they will be safe, like Harriet Tubman did. I find a pit near the river to shit and fill it with my usual mega-colon bowel movement . . . Then I am in a pool where there is a man like Einstein who has been sent to tell me about cosmology and the mysteries of the world. I listen and swim. He speaks of training people to go to the heavenly bodies where disease starts, to see what causes it, how it is kept there. There is something to learn about transport. There is a paradox:

space is nothingness, empty, yet it has the bodies/planets where disease originates. A woman there says the theory will not come for a couple of years. The man was sent to talk just to me but now there are lots of officials around. Someone says that what I missed will be explained in a journal of our new society.

Here the father principle is depotentiated and unconscious. The patriarchal is no longer condemning. Thus the repressed emotionality, passion, and relation to nature, which the dreamer associated to the slaves, can start to move towards freedom. The dream ego acts with the psychopomp Self figure in the underground railroad to free the oppressed shadow. In the process the dreamer can relieve herself of the massive accumulation of impacted aggression—the resentment she had built up as a dutiful family scapegoat.

Then, like a baptism, a new archetypal perspective is opened to her. The extraordinary messenger reveals that disease and evil have a transpersonal source. They belong to the universe, not to her personally. But she is to be involved in the process of comprehending this dark side of cosmic life as part of a developing new dimension of consciousness, a new society. In the dream there are mysteries of "transport" which she explains were "due to centrifugal force, so a special essence carrying people can flow from one cosmic body to another."

This image suggested to her that the energy generated by recircling the life problem through her analysis and her introversion, could permit human consciousness to make the intuitive leap necessary to explore a divine paradox: that out of Nothingness come spheres of matter-energy-awareness that create pain. This suggests a modern equivalent of Buddha's vision. Just as *avidya* (self-delusion) is the cause of suffering, so it is that the partial and distorted consciousness inherent in the complexes we are destined to bear cause dis-ease. Only through the "transport" between these complexes, accomplished by circumambulating the Self's wholeness pattern, can we find the meaning to relativize inevitable human suffering. Evil can thus be seen as related to its transpersonal source.

Service to the scapegoat archetype also serves to differentiate evil, to discriminate between levels of the shadow. Here is a woman's dream that illustrates the need to be aware of the difference between personal, collective, and archetypal shadow contents:

> I have cleaned out my drainpipe and then followed it outside. It leads me to a fertilizer factory. There are pipes from each house in town. All the drainage and shit goes into three large drums and is heated up. Then it gets shoveled out as manure to make farms fertile. There is some left over in the drums—a dark residue. That gets piped through a special direct tube into a hole in the sea.

This woman had discovered that she could not get a revered mentor to accept her when she felt hatred. The hot rage had freed her ego from the idealizing transference and permitted her a view of an alternative mode of handling the unacceptable emotion. She could relate to it consciously and sort out her feelings, even accept some of the shadows from which her mentor turned away. The strong affects could be used as fertilizer for her environment, to make things grow, when she expressed them in dehydrated, conscious form. Some of her resentment was a valid and collective stand against a shallow, sentimental whitewashing of reality. But the deepest residue of the collective shit must go back, as the dream indicates, into the unconscious. Like the ring in Germanic legend and Tolkien's trilogy, such libido is too much to bear and needs to be returned to the unconscious, to the gods. It will return in some new form, for libido does not vanish. But it can not be borne by the individual or by the collective. It cannot be redeemed or changed to detoxify it by any merely human control.

This distinction in levels of the collective shadow is analogous to that made in the occult tradition between relative and absolute evil. There is a part of the shadow that is culturally relative, which when made conscious can be revalued and returned to enrich the collective. There is also an abysmal, even willful destructiveness that would turn against cultural evolution and the gods themselves. This is absolute evil, part of some incomprehensible malevolence and power before which, like Job, we can only cover our mouths when we see it in nature and glimmering darkly in ourselves.

The woman mentioned above saw her hatred of life and destructiveness as related to the energies which produced the concentration camps, as well as to the energies that erupt from the depth of psychosis. Like all scapegoat-identified individuals, she too readily took excessive personal responsibility for these aspects of the collective shadow. She had in fact spent her earlier life in service to causes and in helping others. For her the black hole in the sea seemed connected to the depths of terrible powers—the cleft of Mordor, the archaic, primeval tomb—a black hole which focuses the ineluctable destructiveness of unrelated Being, that darkest coldness. In the dream she could see it was transpersonal.

Looking into the maw of this fierce, fearsome place of power has a dual effect. It is not only tomb, it is also womb. It releases the individual to a new birth. One's own hatred and destructiveness can be seen as a reflection of the dark side of the transpersonal, which for individuals identified with the scapegoat is a necessary affirmation. The shadow energies with which they have been identified, ultimately even the hate and destructiveness they feel, are reflections of the dark side of existence. They can be claimed consciously as affirmations of wholeness and of the Self's capacity to bring forth in each of us our own monstrous individuality. But besides this, recognition of the awesome places of power forces us to take a personal stand. We come into ourselves as we wrestle with the dark energies surging through us and through others, as we learn to stand consciously against the mere acting out of the powers in which we, each of us, partake.

The ancient scapegoat rite stands at the periodic transitions that usher in the New Year. It is a foundation sacrifice to propitiate the divinity and ensure divine protection of the new phase or form of cultural life. The widespread evidence in our time of injury to the deepest and earliest layers of the psyche, and of alienation and rejection–inferiority complexes, suggests that a new age is in preparation, and that we as individuals suffer its formation. Exile from the original nurturing container, concretized in the family collective, is a commonplace in our age.

Such consciousness can only be served individually. Each person destined to become a conscious individual by virtue of exile from the collective comes to a particular view and relation to this consciousness—one fostered in part through one's own life wounds and particular kind of exile. Those who come to this awareness are the builders of a new temple and a new kingdom.[9]

There is a Sufi story that was brought to my attention independently by three analysands identified with the scapegoat archetype. It expresses the positive meaning of the scapegoat as the carrier of a new order.

The Wayward Princess

A certain king believed that what he had been taught, and what he believed, was right. In many ways he was a just man, but he was one whose ideas were limited.

One day he said to his three daughters: "All that I have is yours or will be yours. Through me you obtained your life. It is my will which determines your future, and hence determines your fate."

Dutifully, and quite persuaded of the truth of this, two of the girls agreed.

The third daughter, however, said: "Although my position demands that I be obedient to the laws, I cannot believe that my fate must always be determined by your opinions."

"We shall see about that," said the king.

He ordered her to be imprisoned in a small cell, where she languished for years. Meanwhile the king and his obedient daughters spent freely of the wealth which would otherwise have been expended upon her.

The king said to himself: "This girl lies in prison not by her own will but by mine. This proves, sufficiently for any logical mind, that it is my will, not hers which is determining her fate."

The people of the country, hearing of their princess's situation, said to one another: "She must have done or said something very wrong for a monarch, with whom we find no fault, to treat his own flesh and blood so." For they had not arrived at the point where they felt the need to dispute the king's assumption of rightness in everything.

From time to time the king visited the girl. Although she was pale and weakened from her imprisonment, she refused to change her attitude.

Finally the king's patience came to an end. "Your continued defiance," he said to her, "will only annoy me further, and seem to weaken my rights, if you stay within my realms. I could kill you, but I am merciful. I therefore banish you into the wilderness adjoining my territory. This is a wilderness inhabited only by wild beasts and such eccentric outcasts who cannot survive in our rational society. There you will soon discover whether you can have an existence apart from that of your family; and, if you can, whether you prefer it to ours."

His decree was at once obeyed, and she was conveyed to the borders of the kingdom. The princess found herself set loose in a wild land which bore little resemblance to the sheltered surroundings of her upbringing. But she soon learned that a cave would serve for a house, that nuts and fruit came from trees as well as from golden plates, that warmth came from the Sun. This wilderness had a climate and a way of existing on its own.

After some time she had so ordered her life that she had water from springs, vegetables from the earth, fire from a smoldering tree.

"Here," she said to herself, "is a life whose elements belong together, from a completeness, yet neither individually or collectively do they obey the commands of my father the king."

One day a lost traveler—as it happened a man of great riches and ingenuity—came upon the exiled princess, fell in love with her, and took her back to his own country, where they were married.

After a space of time, the two decided to return to the wilderness where they built a huge and prosperous city where their wisdom, resources and faith were expressed to their fullest possible extent. The "eccentrics" and other outcasts, many of them thought to be madmen, harmonized completely and usefully with this many-sided life.

The city and its surrounding countryside became renowned throughout the entire world. It was not long before its power and beauty far outshone that of the realm of the princess's father. By the unanimous choice of the inhabitants, the princess and her husband were elected to the joint monarchy of this new and ideal kingdom.

At length the king decided to visit this strange and mysterious place which had sprung up in the wilderness, and which was, he heard, peopled at least in part by those whom he and his like despised.

As, with bowed head, he slowly approached the foot of the throne upon which the young couple sat and raised his eyes to meet those whose repute of justice, prosperity and understanding far exceeded his own, he was able to catch the murmured words of his daughter:

"You see, Father, every man and woman has his own fate and his own choice."[10]

In the tale exile provides an impetus to re-sort, reconcile, and redeem the old value system, and permits the establishment of a new kingdom. In this new kingdom the old collective values are left behind—not killed or rebelled against, but simply abandoned, outgrown. And the new kingdom is set up in the wilderness—the in-between place where wanderers and "eccentrics" dwell. The wilderness, an image so frequent in scapegoat-identified individuals' dreams, becomes finally an image of the interface, a ground from which the stable ego can actively seek out a creative relation to the ever-present breadths and depths of the objective psyche.

Radically new in this vision is the respect of each individual for the particularity of another's views and contribution. As one woman put it:

Because I can love my own scars and my strengths now—care about them and parent them—I can even love my own fate. Also I can accept the wounds and strengths in others and forgo needing to be the one who is right and powerful or the one who is wrong and disgustingly weak. We are each right, and each wrong, like the blind men with the elephant. Because we each have a piece of the truth. The truth is there but we are each limited to our own limited view. So we need each other and complement each other.

The scapegoat problem admits of no easy resolution in collective culture. The spirit of all groups is prone to magic-level consciousness, with its propensity for splitting and shadow projection. Most groups retain their shared sense of positive identity by coalescing against an adversary—thrusting out what is felt to be negative—just as most individuals do.[11] But the type of consciousness that permits witnessing this fact is not a characteristic of the primitive group spirit. It must be deliberately fostered. It can only be carried by individuals. Unless there is respect for individual perspectives within the group, the gadfly voices crying in the collective wilderness may go undifferentiated.[12] Objective witnesses cannot then be discriminated from the unadapted cranks, self-seekers, and unconscious borderline characters, who thrive off taking oppositional positions in order to fill their own power needs. Too often the authoritarian hierarchy of the group exacerbates the inherent difficulty of differentiation and quells potentially creative dissent.

The archetype of the scapegoat itself can mediate between a coherent, positively identified group and outsiders, just as it mediates between individual ego ideals and shadow—by making conscious the dynamics and meaning of shadow projection. However, unless the archetype is carried with a bystander awareness that permits disidentification, it will mire group members and the group spirit in splits similar to those suffered by individuals. In order for the archetype to be carried with consciousness, it needs a meaningful image that can contain its splits and hold a mirror up to its own nature.

While Christ is for many Christians merely another scapegoat who will bear all the believer's sins, from an introverted,
spiritual perspective he may be seen as the symbol of one who
bears the suffering of the inner opposites consciously, as his
personal crucifixion. In this sense he is a model for the individuating ego, which bears its wholeness as undefensively—and
hence consciously—as possible.[13] This implies accepting qualities that match the ego ideal as well as those who fall short of
it, holding the opposites together simultaneously, with thought
and intuition, in order to perceive one's self-image. This
permits a disconcerting and sobering view of the paradoxes,
sonorities, and dissonances of one's own nature.

An equally meaningful symbol enabling consciousness of
these oppositions from a feminine, feeling, and rhythmically
alternating perspective may be found in images of the Great
Goddess (e.g., Inanna, Persephone, Kali, Isis). These express
ideal and shadow aspects of the whole, balancing through
time. Thus Inanna is sometimes life-promoting, sometimes
ruthlessly destructive; Kali is sometimes maternal and sometimes savagely devouring. They symbolize a model that permits the individuating ego to experience both sides, or many
sides, of its nature with emotional intensity, and to remember
them all as they manifest on the paradox-containing ground
of time behind the divergences. This model, because it
depends on the integrity of embodied and affectual perception, is time-bound.

Both of these symbolic patterns imply the necessity of coming to an awareness of the ground of reality behind the opposites. They suggest the spiritual awareness of the tree of life
and death, which in legend lies hidden from all but the initi-
ates, encircled behind the tree of the knowledge of good and
evil. To arrive at such awareness involves a transformation in
one's perception of the godhead itself. This transformation is

implicit in the healing of the scapegoat complex, for the function of the two goats, sacrificed to atone with the divinity, is initially carried by the victim-ego and the alienated ego. The hidden, traumatized "true self" is returned to life, as is the burden carrier, through experiences that feel like grace, and through finding access to the parental archetypes in the ritual caldron of analysis. Then the part can heal and develop. But both parts return to life with their extraordinary visions of sacrifice, separation, grief, confusion, sheer emptiness, and evil. They have intimate knowledge of shadow and suffering. Such vision must be integrated into a new concept of reality or the godhead. Only when one's experiences can be seen as meaningfully related to an image of the transpersonal, can the scapegoat-identified individual find the self-acceptance necessary for life. Many such persons come to recognize that the dark side of the godhead is a palpable force—one that merits the respect of conscious confrontation. Within the context of the amoral "phenomenon" of the divinity,[14] the human shadow finds its transpersonal meaning and purpose. It participates in the paradox of divine order and disorder.

Such perception is hard won. It is what the patriarchs of religions shield humankind from knowing when they circumscribe reality and the godhead with the ideals of virtue. Paradoxically, it is also those very virtues, and their companion vices, that create scapegoating and through it the potential development of the consciousness and conscience capable of relating to the reality behind what is called virtue and vice. And the shields themselves are valuable, for only the strong, disciplined, and devoted can bear to penetrate to such paradoxical and painful awareness of the multivalent wholeness of life. Those who suffer the scapegoat complex are among those called to view, which is acquired both through, and in order to find, the healing of the complex.

— An Archetypal Dilemma: —
The LA Riots

JEROME S. BERNSTEIN

THE LOS ANGELES RIOTS OF 1992 shocked not only the nation but the world as well. Those who witnessed the violence firsthand, or who viewed the destruction on television, were subjected to some of the most intense rage, cynicism, and human despair a group of people can feel and express. It is important to note that, although there have been myriad examples of civil disobedience and disruptive demonstration by almost every ethnic and cultural group since colonial times, the nature and intensity of the Los Angeles riots is unprecedented. What's more it is unique to the Black minority in this country. Although the riots reflect patterns we witnessed throughout the 1960s, 1970s, and 1980s, they are the most dramatic and destructive expressions of Black rage and despair we have yet seen in the twentieth century.

Of particular note during this period of American history is that riots by Black citizens across the country (Newark, Detroit, Los Angeles, Washington, D.C., and elsewhere) have been self-destructive. They have all destroyed economic and social structures *within their own ethnic and geographical community.* This characteristic of civil outrage is unique to Black populations of the United States. When other groups have sought to express their outrage through civil disturbance of one sort or another, their acts of dissent, including riots, always have been aimed at the "establishment" or the perceived oppressor group. For Blacks in the United States, the pattern of destroying their own community, their own economic base, their own social services, their own public facilities, their own businesses, their own community infrastructure, and in some cases, even their own homes, is a telltale sign not just of enormous rage but, above all else, of despair and hopelessness. It reflects a kind of hopelessness that no longer discriminates between what is self-destructive and what is destructive of the others. It is as if hopelessness is so profound that there is no longer any concern for the self. Why is this pattern unique to Black Americans?

Not Just Another Minority Group

ALTHOUGH BLACK AMERICANS REPRESENT one of the largest, and certainly the oldest, minority groups in the United States, they have enjoyed the least progress towards full enfranchisement and equality of any other such group, by any measure.[1] Blacks were literally disenfranchised when they were brought here as slaves, and 300 years later all too many of them remain so economically, socially, culturally, or spiritually. That is part of the message of the Los Angeles riots. Ironically, in the case of the 1992 Los Angeles riots, although little noted, the "rioters" were not all poor Blacks, but included some middle-class Blacks as well.

It is hard to imagine the same scenario which led up to the 1992 riots happening with members of any other ethnic or racial group. If Rodney King had been Irish, Jewish, Japanese, Hispanic, or even African, the events that took place would never have unfolded quite the same way. It is my contention that the three police officers who were acquitted in the assault on Rodney King would have been found guilty or at the very least there would have been a plea bargain or a hung jury. This realization is something which almost every Black in this country knows and feels—that Blacks are at the bottom of the heap in terms of civil protections. They are the most discriminated against of any minority in this country. That has been so throughout our history and it remains so today.

Carl Jung's concept of the shadow helps us to realize, upon reflection, that in Western culture, skin color plays a powerful role in the collective projection of our nation's shadow. The darker the skin color, the greater the shadow projections and the worse the discrimination. This is not only true in the United States, but throughout all of Western civilization—witness recent events in Germany and other countries in Europe.[2] In a psycho-spiritual sense, a culture that subscribes to a religious gospel that holds that its principle god is one who ". . . is light and in him is no darkness at all,"[3] very much loads the relative value of light and dark in that society.

Westerners tend to forget that although death and evil are almost universally portrayed as very dark, usually black (e.g., Darth Vader in the "Star Wars" myth), this association is *western*, not archetypal and universal. In many African cultures, for example, dark and evil are portrayed, not surprisingly, as white. The trappings of the shadow are usually opposite to the characteristics of whatever is ego syntonic, that is, they are the opposite of our associations with our ideal self. This is not the result of individual choice but is an archetypal fact. It is a characteristic of the archetype of the shadow.

Thus, in Western culture in general, and in American society in particular, Blacks as a group carry the collective shadow of the culture as a whole. This archetypal fact, in my view, accounts for the extraordinary rage and hopelessness at the core of the collective unconscious of the Black community in this country.

When I was in government and engaged in civil rights work during the 1960s, a familiar slogan often quoted by Black individuals and groups was, "Last hired and first fired." This slogan expressed not only the reality then, but the archetypal reality described above. During the late 1960s, I was a consultant to the model cities program in Miami, Florida, assisting that program with job training and employment efforts on behalf of the Black community. In the course of six months, years of work, and virtually the total employment of Blacks in the tourist industry, were wiped out by the federal government's decision to resettle thousands of Cubans thrown out of Cuba by Castro. The situation for Blacks in the Miami area since that time has changed for the worse. Thousands were forced to relocate just to survive. At the time, the State Department released millions of dollars in "discretionary" funds to train and resettle Cuban nationals, while hard fought for funds earmarked for job training and improving the economic standards of Black citizens were cut and eventually wiped out. At the time, I could not find a single sympathetic ear in Washington. Black Americans in Miami have remained the permanent poverty group ever since.

Taken consciously and sympathetically, our awareness that they have become the archetypal scapegoats of this culture could mark the beginning of our healing a 300-year-old wound still carried in the psyche of all Black Americans. Nothing will heal the alienation within the Black community of this country that does not both recognize *and take responsibility for* the fact that Blacks have been and remain the permanent scapegoat of our culture in ways that are manifested in no other minority group. As important as they are, *nothing*—not social programs, not money, not hiring quotas, not civil rights laws—can heal this wound unless it takes this psychological fact into consideration. Whatever interim healing which might take place can and will be undone, often in a flash, when this crushing fact rams its way through into reality. What happened in Los Angeles in 1992 was not just the result of a few angry people but the eruption of this volatile archetype which we have yet to recognize and appropriately address.

Like Sisyphus pushing his heavy burden up that hill, the boulder soon came crashing down. In 72 hours all the progress we might have believed we made was not only wiped out for the residents of South Central Los Angeles, but indirectly for Black individuals and communities across the country. The dynamics of the shadow archetype are what they are; they cannot be escaped. The only hope we have is to face them—lest the boulder come crashing down on all of us again, Black and non-Black, as it did on that spring day in Los Angeles. There cannot be effective long-term healing between the Black community and the dominant culture without major psychological adjustment in the perception of Black culture and the feelings of alienation which lie at the deepest levels in that group. Feelings of benevolence, social equality, and the pursuit of greater civil liberties and equal justice, although essential, will not be sufficient. The lesson of the Los Angeles riots is that there is an archetypally derived, permanent, and silent stream of alienation, rage, and hopelessness which runs at the deepest levels in the Black community, and it is constantly eroding the very foundation upon which all efforts to improve social justice are built.

The problem can be cast as one of no hope for redemption deep in the psyche of the Black minority group. That is because the "original sin" literally is not theirs. It was perpetuated on them by slave traders of centuries past, not a sin committed by them. As the archetypal scapegoat of the dominant culture, they remain caught in a dilemma from which there is seemingly no escape, where virtually all the cards are in the hands of the perceived persecutor. As long as they are the scapegoats the Black community will remain the outcast of the nation, forever used to carry the country's sins. Having been cut off from their roots, with literally no place to go, the disenfranchised are strongly predisposed to rebel against their assigned role with violent rage.

A comparison with the drama of the Black disenfranchisement in South Africa is quite telling. The power problem is radically different between Black Americans and South African Blacks. The latter *will* win, ultimately—not only because moral consciousness is on their side, but out of sheer numbers. They are not a minority. They so dramatically outnumber their white rulers that the tables will be turned—military intervention by other western nations being a possibility now virtually ruled out by the growth of moral consciousness in the western psycho-political process.

The other significant difference between American Blacks and South African Blacks is that the latter still live on their own soil, are not cut off from their cultural, religious, and psychic (tribal) roots, as are American Blacks. They have a psychic and cultural heritage that sustains and feeds them and that, no matter how disenfranchised they are, has given them a sense of sustained self-definition and pride. Ultimately they retain sufficient psychological, moral, and latent political power, which is enabling them to reject the projection of original sin from the white minority in their country.

On the other hand, the American Black, particularly those who are disenfranchised (e.g., urban ghetto youth), has been cut off from those cultural and psychic roots for over 300 years and has lived permanently not only as a minority, but with the realization that the only power which he/she can truly have is that which is permitted (bestowed). This is tantamount to power without title. Archetypally, at a collective level, it almost always takes power to reverse a projection, that is, to give back a projection. That is the present dilemma of Black Americans, unlike South African Blacks.

What Can Be Done?

FROM A PSYCHOLOGICAL OR ARCHETYPAL POINT OF VIEW, *both* the oppressed and the oppressor are victims, though obviously in different ways and with different severity. As an archetypal phenomenon, shadow projection takes place in the absence of conscious control. Thus, although few white Americans would deny that racial discrimination is illegal, if not immoral, they continue to project the scapegoat onto Black Americans. It is not that no one cares. It is that they are caught up in a psychological phenomenon that few people in our society understand.

Although I grew up in a predominantly Black neighborhood, and have always felt comfortable with Blacks, I still catch myself unconsciously projecting onto them. Although I understand the phenomenon of projection, it still catches me short when I find myself doing it.

Archetypally, the scapegoat is only a portion of an important ritual. In the Old Testament, the scapegoat (an actual goat) was banished into the desert to die, representing sins the community needed to reject and push out. Afterwards, the temple priests took the best goats or lambs of the community and offered them as a ritual to the godhead as a "sin offering." The latter was a way of both acknowledging and atoning for the sins of the community. Oftentimes, as in the Hebraic rite of

Yom Kippur, the Day of Atonement, the community, collectively and individually, would *explicitly* acknowledge and atone for its sins.[4]

This is the missing piece necessary to begin a lasting healing process and to address the psychological dynamics that led up to the Los Angeles riots of 1992. Without this "sin offering," the banishment and atonement is incomplete. And, most important, the community, individually and collectively, does not take conscious responsibility for its literal sins. Inevitably, the same sins get projected onto other individuals or groups—merely reassigning the role of scapegoat.

It is noteworthy that only one[5] of the politicians who addressed the tragedy in South Central Los Angeles spoke to the underlying feelings and emotions that led to the riots. *None* of them addressed the psychological dynamics that gave rise to what happened. Although lip service was paid to the anger associated with the acquittal of the three policemen in the Rodney King assault, no one even attempted to explore the depth of alienation and despair this event triggered in the Black community. And no one addressed the roots of that despair. And certainly, no politician ever addressed the archetypal issues. No one made a "sin offering" in the name of the dominant culture, seeking to heal Black disenfranchisement and alienation within our society. At this point there are few who even perceive it.

The closest thing to such a "sin offering" in this country was the 1968 Kerner Commission Report, which spoke dramatically and eloquently to the problem of a nation divided against itself. It acknowledged the evils of racism and discrimination and recommended massive programs to improve conditions in the ghettos and thus speed efforts toward a truly integrated society. The report, considered to be one of the most comprehensive and serious attempts to deal with racial tensions in this country, was left to languish by the Nixon and other administrations. Although the Kerner Commission Report was comprehensive and forward looking, it lacked, not surprisingly, the archetypal insights outlined above. We were not sufficiently developed, neither individually nor collectively, to embrace the underlying problem in all its archetypal realities. I don't know if we are ready for that even now.

What Might a Sin Offering Look Like?

THE ENACTMENT OF NATIONAL LEGISLATION making Martin Luther King's birthday a national holiday has led to significant curriculum changes in many schools. On that holiday there is a focus on the civil rights movement in this country. Similarly, we see themes of racial discrimination making their way into popular movies and TV programs. To complete the cycle, however, we need a theme of reconciliation. An effort to integrate psychological material that addresses the archetypal underpinnings of prejudice could become the collective "sin offering" that we need in this country. It is important to recognize that in order to have a complete healing, a "sin offering" must be made by *both* the white and Black communities. The dominant culture must acknowledge that Blacks carry a special burden, being the only minority group in this country that did not initially choose to come here and which was forced to stay and suffer the profound indignity of slavery. Whites would have to stop blaming Blacks for their psychohistorical legacy and be willing to acknowledge that indeed a "sin" was committed and is perpetuated through contemporary racism, e.g., the Rodney King police trial.

I am reminded of one of the greatest acts of statesmanship of the 20th century. In one of the last interviews before his assassination, Anwar Sadat was asked about the inherent mistrust of Arabs by Jews. He answered that he understood the sensitivity and mistrust of Jews, given what was done to them during World War II. It was a single, simple, feeling statement that carried no overt political import whatsoever. And yet it was one of the most politically ethical and powerful statements ever made by a head of state. The impact was profoundly healing. If only President Bush had made a similar empathic statement on his tour of the Los Angeles riot scene. As it was, his central message was that he would beef up police protection in the area.

The Black community must come to the point where it is willing to consciously let go of its condemnation of white society. Unless the Black community can do that, whites will be held in perpetual sin without the hope of redemption, just as Blacks have been held in the position of permanent scapegoats by whites. If either community clings to holding the other in perpetual sin or scapegoatism, all hope for healing is aborted. Moreover, both sides must make the "sin offerings" simultaneously. For one side to say to the other, "You go first because you have perpetuated the greater sin," will also abort the process.

For such an approach to be effective, there would have to be a commission, composed of Blacks and whites, which would begin to focus on specific archetypal dynamics. My fantasy is that there would be a large round table and at its center there would be a large effigy of a goat—one side black, the other side white. This goat would be there throughout the entire process to symbolize *and remind* participants that the core problem they are addressing is an archetypal one. And it would be made clear that the "problems" of the past have really been symptoms of this core archetypal problem now being addressed.

One final but important dynamic in the American political process should be mentioned. It is my contention that within the collective unconscious there is a powerful drive for a moral consciousness. This has been evidenced over the past several decades through the vehicle of the Cold War and the transcendent function of the collective unconscious. The upshot of all this has been the birth of a moral consciousness as an overt and powerful dynamic in world politics. Ironically, this new psychodynamic in world politics was brought along by the terrible threat of nuclear annihilation. Throughout the Cold War that threat appears to have awakened us, in the deepest possible way, to a new and profound reverence for the sacredness of life. The tension of these years has literally constellated what Jung called "the transcendent function," giving rise to a moral consciousness that has outlived the Cold War.[6]

In spite of the active transcendent function emerging in international politics, the domestic progress of the United States has been pathologically stuck since the 1970s. For decades we were so focused on the Soviet Union as the evil empire that we became dissociated from our own shadow. As a result we have domestically moved along on the waves of greed and increasing mean-spiritedness. We have blinded ourselves to the plight of our fellow citizens, are callous toward the increasing hordes of homeless people living and dying in our city streets. Although we may be able to catch fleeting glimpses of moral consciousness struggling to take the country to a higher plane, the transformative process seems to bog down in political name-calling. Political transformation seems elusive, indeed.

At the opposite pole from the archetype of moral consciousness is psychopathy. "Psychopathy" refers to those individuals ". . . who are ill primarily in terms of society and of conformity with social, cultural, and *ethical* demands."[7,8] I believe this definition applies not only to individuals but to certain aspects of the political process within the United States. At the level of the collective unconscious, the American political process is caught up in a critical struggle between these two archetypal poles—psychopathy and transcendence.

It might be instructive to look at how the psychopathic process was manifested in the context of the Los Angeles riots. First, the president of our country generally mirrors the values of the national psyche. Given this assumption, consider what President Bush mirrored in his initial response to the Rodney King acquittals. What did his responses tell us about our country's psychopathy?

On the evening of April 29, 1992, in the wake of the announcement that the jury had acquitted three of the four defendants accused of beating Rodney King, President Bush stated: ". . . the court system has worked; what's needed now is calm, respect for the law. . . ." (as reported by William Raspberry in the *Washington Post*, May 1, 1992, p. A27). That was followed 48 hours later by a more conciliatory speech and meetings with civil rights leaders, one more carefully crafted by the president's speech writers and other spin doctors. But it was too late. As we learn in the clinical professions, the first words out of our mouths are usually the inner truth—though often a truth we would rather not reveal. And those first words of George Bush on the evening of April 29, 1992, reflected a psychopathy. His message that day was that the wanton beating of Rodney King, which we saw replayed over and over again on national TV, simply didn't happen. His call for respect for the law, even in the wake of such a blatant trampling of justice, was a mockery of the very concept. Beyond that, there was the implication that the injury to Blacks doesn't matter to the white community.

When Bush finally visited the Los Angeles devastation, he appeared to be moved by the experience.[9] But none of that prevented his taking the opportunity to do a bit of negative campaigning, using the crisis to win (he hoped) a few votes for the upcoming presidential election. He identified *all* the rioters as "looters," law-breakers who had no right to demonstrate against the power structure. He thereby obfuscated a legitimate sense of moral outrage and social injustice experienced by Black and non-Black communities all across the nation. George Bush's comments were not merely political rhetoric; they also demonstrated dangerous dissociative behavior, in an extreme form and characteristic of the psychopathic process.

When viewed from an archetypal vantage point, the psychodynamics of the Los Angeles riots give us cause for despair—and for hope. Which one we end up with depends on how much we struggle to bring full consciousness to the deeper layers of the problem. Much depends on how much responsibility we are willing to take for our shadow.

PART VIII

Shadow Poetics

Anger Against Children
Robert Bly

The vet screams, and throws his crutch at a passerby.
"Hey lady you want to meet a child-killer?"
African drums play all night for the women
With their heads down on motel tables.
Parents take their children into the deepest Oregon forests,
And leave them there. When the children
Open the lunchbox, there are stones inside, and a note saying,
  "Do your own thing."
And what would the children do if they found their way home
  in the moonlight?
The planes have already landed on Maui, the parents are on
  vacation.
Our children live with a fear at school and in the house.
The mother and father do not protect the younger child from
  the savagery of the others.
Parents don't want to face the children's rage,
Because the parents are also in rage.

What is it like to have stayed this long in civilization—
To have witnessed the grave of Tutankamen open once more?
What is it like to wear sweatshirts and bluejeans
And wait for hours to see the bracelets of those wasteful death-
  coddlers,
Who learned to conquer conscious life?
What is it like to have the dynamo, the light-bulb, the
  Parliamentary system, the electrical slaves embedded in
  elevator doors,
The body scanners that see sideways, the extravagant and
  elegant fighters,
And still be unconscious? What is that like?

Well of course there is rage.
The thirty-four year old mother
Wants to reject the child still in the womb,
And she asks Senators to pass laws to prevent that.
The husband dreams of killing his wife, and the wife lays
    plots.
She imagines that he is an Oppressor,
And that she is an Aztec Princess.
In the night she holds an obsidian knife over her husband's
    sleeping body.
He dreams he is a deer being torn apart by female demons.

This is the rage that shouts at children.
This is the rage that cannot be satisfied,
Because each year more ancient Chinese art objects go on
    display,
So the rage goes inward at last,
It ends in doubt, in self-doubt, dyeing the hair, and love of
    celebrities.
The rage comes to rest at last in the talk show late at night,
When the celebrities without anger or grief tell us that only
    the famous are good, only they live well.
There are waifs inside us, broken by the Pauline gospels;
We know them,
And those who step on desire as a horse steps on a chick.
No cry comes out, only silence, and the faint whisper of the
    collapsing birdskull.

Here the sleepers sleep, here the Rams and the Bears play.
The old woman weeps at night in her room at the Nursing
    Facility.
There are no bridges over the ocean.

She sees a short dock, and ahead of that darkness, hostile
    waters, lifting swells,
Fitfully lit, or not lit at all.
Tadpoles drowse in the stagnant holes.
The gekko goes back to his home in the cold rain.

The wife of the Chrysler dealer is in danger of being
    committed again.
She left the hospital hopeful, she struggles hard,
She reads Laing and Rollo May;
But nothing works, she dreams she is interred in Burma.
Cars go past her house at night, Japanese soldiers at the wheel.
Nothing can be done, the kernel opens, all is swept away;
She is carried out of sight.
The doctor arrives; once more she leaves dry-eyed for the
    hospital.

I am twenty-eight again. I sleep curled up,
My fingers widen as I sleep, my toes grow immense at night.
Tears flow; I am in some bin apart from him I love.

The ocean king, his ship sunk, lies alone on his bed.
His interior engine has been catapulted into fragments,
Valves and drive shaft scattered, the engine mount settles to
    sand.
The saddened king goes about, all night he reaches down,
Picking up bolts from the sand, and piston rings; by morning
    all is scattered again.

We wake, no dream is remembered, the scenes gone into
    smoke.
We are in some enormous place, abandoned,

Where Adam Kadmon has been forgotten, the luminous man
    is dissolved.
The sarcophagus contains the rotted bones of the monks; so
    many lived in the desert.
None are alive, only the bones lie in the dust.
My friend goes to Philadelphia to claim his father's body.
It lies in an uncarpeted room in the ghetto, there was no one
    else to claim the body.
The time of manifest destiny is over, the time of grief has
    come.

Meditations on the Insatiable Soul
Robert Bly

1.

The man who sits up late at night cutting
His nails, the backs of black whales, the tip
Of the mink's tail, the tongue that slips out of lips, all of these
Testify to a soul used to eating and being eaten.
Urged on by the inner pressure of teeth,
Some force, animal-born, is slippery, edgy,
Impatient, greedy to pray for new heavens,
Unforgiving, resentful, like a fire in dry wood.

2.

Greeks sit by the fire cleaning their bright teeth.
Let Portia grieve in her sorrowing house.
Let blackbirds come. The insatiable soul
Begins to eat shellfish, the Caribbean islands,
The rainforests, Amazon. Who wants the meat cooked
In the Holocaust? Oh, you know.
The traveller asleep in Charlemagne's cave
Laughs in his murky unshaven dream.

3.

Some ill-smelling, libidinous, worm-shouldered
Deep-reaching desirousness rules the countryside.
Let sympathy pass, a stranger, to other shores!
Let the love between men and women be ground up
And fed to the talk shows! Let every female breast
Be photographed! Let the father be hated! Let the son be
   hated!
Let twelve-year-olds kill the twelve-year-olds!
The Great Lord of Desirousness ruling all.

4.

The shingled hawk lives with her ear to the tree.
The mouse unerringly feels the immensity.
"By Gor, I will not consent to die this day."
But she steps out into the air. And she is gone.
What will you say of the Hundred Years' War,
But that, Melancthon and Augustine aside,
Some element, Dresdenized, coated with Somme
Mud and flesh entered, and all prayer was vain.

5.

Northern lights illumine the storm-troll's house.
There men murdered by God promenade.
The buffalo woman plays her bony flute calling
The lonely father trampled by the buffalo god.
The foreskin of angels shelter the naked cradle.
The stew of discontents feeds the loose souls.
And the owl husbands the moors, harries the mouse,
Beforehand, behindhand, with his handsome eyes.

Notes

Part I
Shadow and Culture

1. C. G. Jung, *The Collected Works of C.G. Jung* (hereafter denoted as *CW*) (Princeton: Princeton University Press; Bollingen Series, vol. 8., 1969), § 607–610, 615–618.

2. Liliane Frey-Rohn, *From Freud to Jung: A Comparative Study of the Psychology of the Unconscious* (Boston: Shambhala Publications, 1974), p. 60.

3. Jung, "On the Psychology of the Unconscious," *CW*, vol. 7, p. 66, n 5.

4. Jung, *CW*, vol. 16, §470.

5. Jung, "The Philosophical Tree," *CW*, vol. 13, §335.

6. Jung, "On the Nature of the Psyche" *CW,* vol. 8, § 409.

7. Gustav Fechner, "The Shadow is Alive" (trans. Stephen Simmer), *Spring 51* (1991) p. 85.

8. Frey-Rohn, pp. 59–60.

9. This is Edward Whitmont's phrase. See his article "Individual Transformation and Personal Responsibility" in *Quadrant*, vol. 18, no. 2 (Fall 1985).

10. D. Patrick Miller, "What the Shadow Knows: An Interview with John A. Sanford," *The Sun*, 1989.

11. Robert Bly, *A Little Book on the Human Shadow*, ed. William Booth (San Franciso: HarperCollins, 1988), p. 18.

12. Robert Johnson, *Owning Your Own Shadow* (San Francisco: HarperCollins, 1991), p. 5.

13. Jung in a BBC interview with John Freeman, 1959. See *C.G. Jung Speaking*, eds. McGuire and Hull (Princeton: Princeton University Press; Bollingen Series, 1977), p. 436.

14. Jeremiah Abrams and Connie Zweig, *Meeting the Shadow: The Hidden Power of the Dark Side of Human Nature* (Los Angeles: Jeremy P. Tarcher, Inc., 1991).

15. The example cited is found in Jerome Bernstein's *Power and Politics: The Psychology of Soviet-American Partnership* (Boston: Shambhala Publications, 1989).

Part II
Shadow Awareness

1. Marie-Louise von Franz, *Psychotherapy* (Boston: Shambhala Publications, 1993), pp. 194–95.

2. von Franz, p. 195.

3. C. G. Jung, *CW*, vol. 9, part II, *Aion* (Princeton: Princeton University Press; Bollingen Series, 1959), p. 8.

4. Richard Wilhelm, *I Ching: The Book of Changes*, trans. (Princeton: Princeton University Press; Bollingen Series XIX, 1950) , Hexagram 5, Hsü, Waiting (Nourishment), p.

5. Jack Kornfield, *A Path with Heart* (New York: Bantam Books, 1993), p. 84.

Part III
Between Masculine and Feminine

1. June Singer, "The Age of Androgyny," *Quadrant* (Winter 1975), p. 80.

2. Robert Johnson, *Owning Your Own Shadow* (San Francisco: HarperCollins, 1991), p. 8., see also p. 46.

3. Susan B. Anthony, speech in San Francisco California, July 1871.

4. Mary Wollstonecraft, *A Vindication of the Rights of Women*, ed. Carol Postman (New York: W.W. Norton, 1975), p. 62.

5. Betty Friedan, *The Feminine Mystique* (New York: Dell Publishing Co., 1974).

6. Camille Paglia, San Francisco *Examiner*, July 7, 1991 *Image*, p. 11.

7. Marion Woodman, *The Ravaged Bridegroom; Masculinity in Women* (Toronto: Inner City Books, 1990), p. 18.

8. Barbara Walker, *The Woman's Encyclopedia of Myths and Secrets.* (San Francisco: Harper and Row, 1983), p. 399.

9. Walker, p. 393.

10. Aaron Kipnis, *Knights Without Armor: A Practical Guide for Men in Quest of Masculine Soul* (Los Angeles: Jeremy P. Tarcher Inc., 1991; Putnam, 1992).

11. Murray A. Straus, "Physical Assaults by Wives: A Major Social Problem," *Current Controversies on Family Violence*, eds. R. J. Gelles and D. Loseke (Beverly Hills: Sage, 1993).

12. U. S. Department of Commerce: Bureau of the Census, *Statistical Abstract of the United States: The National Data Book.* 110th ed. (Washington, D.C.: USGPO, 1992); Source Book of Criminal Justice Statistics, U.S. Department of Justice, Bureau of Justice Statistics (Washington, D.C.: USGPO, 1990).

13. Ellen Bass and Laura Davis, *The Courage to Heal: A Guide for Women Survivors of Child Sexual Abuse* (New York: Harper and Row, 1986), pp. 96,198; K. Singer, "Group work with men who experienced incest in childhood," *American Journal of Orthopsychiatry* (July 1989), 59 (3), 466; S. Obrian, *Child Abuse: A Crying Shame* (Provo: Brigham Young University Press, 1980).

14. Erich Neumann, *The Great Mother: An Analysis of the Archetype,* trans. Ralph Mamheim (Princeton: Princeton University Press; Bollingen Series XLVII, 1963). p. 187.

15. Sheila Moon, *Changing Woman and Her Sisters* (San Francisco: Guild for Psychological Studies, 1984), pp. 93–95.

16. Moon, p. 77.

17. Moon, p. 85.

18. Herb Goldberg, *The New Male* (New York: The New American Library, Inc., 1979), p. 145.

19. *Los Angeles Times,* January 19, 1992.

20. Kipnis, *Knights.*

21. Robert Johnson, *Ecstasy: Understanding the Psychology of Joy* (San Francisco: Harper and Row, 1987), p. 46.

22. Sylvia Perera, *The Scapegoat Complex: Toward a Mythology of Shadow and Guilt* (Toronto: Inner City Books, 1986), p. 18.

23. Johnson, *Ecstasy,* p. 43.

Part IV
Sexuality

1. Anthony Stevens, *Archetypes: A Natural History of the Self* (New York: Quill, 1983), p. 213–214.

2. Adolf Guggenbühl-Craig, "Puritanism," in *Psychic Reality and the Spirit of Jung in the 1990's,* Proceedings of the National Conference of Jungian Analysts, Los Angeles, 1990.

3. James Hillman & Wilhelm Roscher, *Pan and the Nightmare* (Dallas, TX: Spring Publications, 1977), p. xiii.

4. Ibid., p. xxv.

5. Robert Stein, *Incest and Human Love: The Betrayal of the Soul in Psychotherapy* (Dallas, TX: Spring Publications, 1984).

6. C. G. Jung, *CW,* vol. 14, § 664.

7. Peter Rutter, *Sex in the Forbidden Zone* (Los Angeles: Jeremy P. Tarcher Inc., 1989).

8. Ibid., p. 4.

9. Ibid., p. 5.

10. Ibid., pp. 5–6.

11. D. H. Lawrence, "A Propos of Lady Chatterley's Lover," in *Sex, Literature and Censorship* (New York: Twayne Publishers, 1953), pp. 92–3.

12. Hillman and Roscher, op. cit., p.xli and p.xliii.

13. D. H. Lawrence, "Benjamin Franklin" in *Essays in Classical American Literature* (New York: Viking Press, 1964), p. 19.

Part V
Addiction

1. Kirk J. Schneider, *Horror and the Holy: Wisdom Teachings of the Monster Tale* (La Salle, IL: Open Court Publishing Co., 1993), p. 65.

2. C. G. Jung, *Letters* 1951–1961 (Princeton: Princeton University Press; Bollingen Series), p. 623–24., in a letter to Bill W., founder of Alcoholics Anonymous.

3. Jung, *CW*, vol. 9, part II, *Aion* (Princeton: Princeton University Press; Bollingen Series, 1959), § 95.

4. Father George Capsanis, *The Eros of Repentance* (Newbury, MA: Praxis Institute Press).

5. C. G. Jung, *CW*, vol. 11, *Answer to Job*, (Princeton: Princeton University Press; Bollingen Series, 1959), § 664.

6. Fred Alan Wolf, *Taking the Quantum Leap* (New York: Harper and Row, 1981), pp. 105–15, 169–75.

7. Marie Louise von Franz, *Projection and Re-Collection in Jungian Psychology* (La Salle, IL: Open Court, Publishing Co., 1980), p. 123, p 116.

8. Jung, *CW* vol. 6, § 708.

9. Jacqueline Small, *Awakening in Time: The Journey from Codependency to Co-Creation* (New York: Bantam Books, 1991).

10. John Conger, *Jung and Reich: The Body as Shadow* (Berkeley, CA: North Atlantic Books, 1988).

11. See especially Stanislav Grof, *The Adventures of Self-Discovery* (Albany, NY: State University of New York, 1988); Thomas Verny with John Kelly, *Secret Life of the Unborn Child* (New York: Dell Publishing Co.Inc., 1988).

Part VI
Money

1. Vivienne Pinto and Warren Roberts, *Complete Poems of D. H. Lawrence* (New York: Viking Press, 1964), p. 522.

2. William H. Desmonde, *Magic, Myth and Money* (New York: Free Press, 1962), pp. 20–25, as quoted by Jacob Needleman in *Money and the Meaning of Life* (New York: Doubleday & Co., 1991).

3. Adolf Guggenbühl-Craig, "Projections: Soul and Money," in *Soul and Money* (Dallas, TX: Spring Publications, 1982), p. 88–89.

Part VII
Prejudice

PERERA

1. Mary Douglas, *Purity and Danger: An Analysis of Concepts of Pollution and Taboo* (London: Routledge & Kegan Paul, 1966) p. 53.

2. Jerome Kagan, "The Parental Love Trap," *Psychology Today* (August 1978), p. 54.

3. Matthew 5:48, King James Version.

4. Jung, *Mysterium Coniunctionis, CW,* vol.14, §117.

5. Jung, "The Fight with the Shadow," *CW*, vol. 10, § 456.

6. Erich Neumann, *Depth Psychology and a New Ethic* (New York: G.P. Putnam's Sons, 1969) p. 130.

7. Judges 5:24, Jerusalem Bible.

8. Neumann, *Depth Psychology*, p. 103.

9. See Edward F. Edinger, *The Creation of Consciousness: Jung's Myth for Modern Man* (Toronto: Inner City Books, 1984), p. 11.

10. Idris Shad, *Tales of the Dervishes* (New York: Dutton, 1969), pp. 63–65.

11. Even groups that start as task-oriented fall into the more primitive form when their cooperative focus becomes blurred or so complex that fractions form around its implementation, or when they become so large that members cannot share with each other in order to find areas of undefensive mutuality and respect.

12. See Edward C. Whitmont, *Return of the Goddess* (New York: Crossroad, 1982), pp. 255–56, and "Individual Transformation and Personal Responsibility," *Quadrant*, vol. 19, no. 1 (Spring, 1986). He suggests the necessity of new forms of group self-confrontation through the mutual "leveling" of individual members. The literature on group and family dynamics supports both the efficacy of such forms and the potential for learning new modes of consciousness through group and family therapy.

13. See Edward F. Edinger, "Christ as Paradigm of the Individuating Ego," *Ego and Archetype: Individuation and the Religious Function of the Psyche* (New York: G.P. Putnam's Sons, 1972).

14. See Jung, "Answer to Job," *Psychology and Religion: West and East, CW* vol. 11, § 600. Yahweh's behavior towards Job, writes Jung, is that of "an unconscious being who cannot be judged morally. Yahweh is a *phenomenon* and, as Job says, 'not a man.'"

BERNSTEIN

1. My comments in this paper about Black Americans are general-
   izations about a group of citizens, in so far as they constitute a
   minority group within the larger culture. Obviously there are
   individual exceptions, even exceptions within subgroups of the
   larger group.

2. One could even conjecture whether history would have turned
   out dramatically different if there was a sufficient number of
   Blacks in Europe during the rise of Nazism to have caught the
   collective shadow projection of Western culture. The current
   resurgence of anti-semitism in Europe is being overshadowed
   by attacks on "foreigners," even in Germany, the darkest foreigners getting the brunt of the assaults.

3. *Revised Standard Version of the New Testament*, John 1:6.

4. See Sylvia Brinton Perera, *The Scapegoat Complex: Toward a
   Mythology of Shadow and Guilt* (Toronto: Inner City Books,
   1986).

5. Representative Maxine Waters (D). from Los Angeles.

6. For a discussion of the development of moral consciousness as a
   major political force in world politics, see Jerome S. Bernstein,
   "Jung, Jungians and the Nuclear Peril," *Psychological
   Perspectives*, vol. 16, no. 1 (1985), pp. 29–39; "Power and Politics
   in the Thermonuclear Age: A Depth-Psychological Approach,"
   Quadrant vol.18, no. 2 (Fall 1985); *Power and Politics: the
   Psychology of Soviet-American Partnership* (Boston: Shambhala
   Publications, 1989); "Victory in Iraq?" *Psychological Perspectives*
   vol. 24 (Spring/Summer 1991); "The Transcendent Function
   and the Collective Unconscious," *Transformation*, C. G. Jung
   Institute of Chicago, June 1992, Issue on the Transcendent
   Function; and "Beyond the Personal: Analytical Psychology
   Applied to Groups and Nations" in *Carl Gustav Jung: Critical*

Assessments, edited by Renos Papadopoulos, 4 vols., (London: Routledge & Kegan Paul, 1993).

7. Robert J. Campbell, *Psychiatric Dictionary*, 6th ed., (London: Oxford University Press. (Italics added.)

8. J. Reid Meloy, *The Psychopathic Mind: Origins, Dynamics and Treatment* (Northvale, NJ: Jason Aronson Inc., 1992), p. 5 defines psychopathy as "a deviant developmental disturbance characterized by an inordinate amount of instinctual aggression and the absence of an object relational capacity to bond. Psychopathy is a process: a continuous interplay of factors and operations that are implicitly progressing or regressing toward a particular end point . . . , *a fundamental disidentification with humanity*." (Italics added.)

9. I would apply this argument to both candidates in the 1992 election. It took Bill Clinton three days to arrive at the riot scene—presumably after he and his political advisers had deemed it politically safe and strategic to do so. The thinking function apparently prevailed over the feeling function and moral consciousness in the Clinton political camp. Such a lack of haste was certainly not motivated by a commitment to moral consciousness which would dictate immediate action on the basis of the human tragedy itself, irrespective of the political fallout from such action.

I have focused here on President Bush's behavior because he was the president and his behavior seems more unambivalently psychopathic than that of Bill Clinton who at times seems to be in a struggle with his own political advisers for control of his soul.

For those who may have watched the testimony of the president's son, Neil Bush, before the Senate Banking Committee regarding his role as a board member in one of the largest bank failures in the nation's history, it was apparent that he literally could not begin to grasp even the most fundamental concept of ethics and conflict of interest. From a clinical standpoint, it was one of the most poignant displays of psychopathic behavior I have ever seen—one that could be a textbook example of the very meaning of psychopathic behavior. Although one could understand the instinct of parents to love and protect a son, one can but wonder what George and Barbara Bush really perceived and what they said to their son in private. Their only statement on the matter was that Neil Bush was being hounded because he was the president's son.

The Contributors

Jeremiah Abrams, LCSW(MA) has worked for the past 24 years as a Jungian therapist, dream analyst, writer, counselor, teacher, and consultant. He is the author of the collected volume *Reclaiming the Inner Child*, and coauthor of the collection *Meeting the Shadow: The Hidden Power of the Dark Side of Human Nature*. He is director of the Mt. Vision Institute in Sausalito, California. In 1992, Jeremiah organized the conference "The Shadow in America," which led to the creation of the present volume.

Jerome S. Bernstein, M.A.P.C. is a Jungian analyst and clinical psychologist in private practice in Santa Fe, New Mexico. He was an official in the United States Office of Economic Opportunity and a consultant to the mayor of New York City, to the governor of New Jersey, and to the chairman of the Navajo Indian tribe. Jerome is the author of *Power and Politics: The Psychology of Soviet-American Partnership*.

Patricia Berry, Ph.D. is president of the Inter-Regional Society of Jungian Analysts. She received her Diplomate from the C. G. Jung Institute, Zürich, and is a practicing Jungian analyst in Cambridge, Massachusetts. Pat is the author of numerous essays, some of which have been collected in her book, *Echo's Subtle Body*.

Robert Bly has had a tremendous influence on contemporary poetry as poet, editor, and translator. He received the National Book Award for his book *Light Around the Body*. His anthology of contemporary and classic poetry, *News of the Universe: poems of twofold consciousness*, is a major contribution bridging psychology and poetics. Bly has written on psychological and mythological themes, most notably in *A Little Book on the Human Shadow* and *Iron John: A Book About Men*.

Elizabeth Herron, M.A. is a writer, consultant, and educator with extensive experience in the area of women's empowerment and gender reconciliation. She is codirector of the Santa Barbara Institute for Gender Studies, and coauthor of the book, *Gender War, Gender Peace: The Quest for Justice Between Men and Women*.

Aaron Kipnis, Ph.D. is codirector of the Santa Barbara Institute for Gender Studies. He has taught depth psychology for 20 years, and is a regular lecturer on male psychology, gender issues, and substance abuse recovery. Aaron is the author of *Knights Without Armor: A Practical Guide for Men in Quest of Masculine Soul,* and coauthor of *Gender War, Gender Peace: The Quest for Justice Between Men and Women.*

Thomas Moore, Ph.D. lecturer, writer and psychotherapist, is the author of *Soul Mates; Care of the Soul; The Planets Within; Rituals of the Imagination; Dark Eros;* and the editor of *A Blue Fire.*

Sylvia Brinton Perera is the author of *Descent to the Goddess: A Way of Initiation for Women, The Scapegoat Complex: Toward a Mythology of Shadow and Guilt,* and coauthor of *Dreams: A Portal to the Source.* Sylvia is a Jungian analyst practicing in New York City, where she teaches at the C. G. Jung Institute.

Robert J. Sardello, Ph.D. is a faculty member of the Dallas (Texas) Institute of Humanities and Culture, and the Chalice of Repose Project in Missoula, Montana. He is former chairman of the Department of Psychology, University of Dallas and has been a practicing Jungian and Archetypal psychotherapist for 20 years. Bob is author of *Facing the World with Soul: The Reimagination of Modern Life* and *Soul Tasks of the Future.*

Jacquelyn Small, MSSW, CSW is the founding director of Eupsychia Institute in Austin Texas. She conducts workshops and seminars around the country. Jacquie's books include *Becoming Naturally Therapeutic: A Return to the True Essence of Helping; Awakening in Time; Transformers, the Artists of Self-Creation;* and *Embodying Spirit: Coming Alive with Meaning and Purpose.*

Robert M. Stein, M.D. is a Jungian analyst and physician who received his training in Zürich while Jung was still alive and giving seminars. He has lectured internationally and his book, *Incest and Human Love: The Betrayal of the Soul in Psychotherapy,* has become a classic which has been translated into many other languages.

Permissions and Copyrights

"**The Shadow in America**," is an original essay by Jeremiah Abrams, delivered as the keynote address at the conference, "The Shadow in America," August, 1992, Omega Institute. Portions of this essay have appeared in the British journal, *I-to-I*. Copyright © 1992, 1993 by Jeremiah Abrams.

"**Light and Shadow**," is an original essay by Patricia Berry, conceived for and presented at the conference, "The Shadow in America," August, 1992, Omega Institute. Copyright © 1992 by Patricia Berry. Used by permission of the author.

"**Gender Wars: Facing the Masculine and Feminine Shadow**," is adapted for this volume from the authors' work-in-progress (Chapter 6), *Gender War, Gender Peace: The Quest for Justice Between Women and Men* by Aaron Kipnis and Elizabeth Herron (New York: William Morrow and Co., 1994). Copyright © 1993 by Aaron Kipnis and Elizabeth Herron. Used by permission of the authors.

"**Sexuality, Shadow, and the Holy Bible**," is an original essay by Robert M. Stein, conceived for and presented at the conference, "The Shadow in America," August, 1992, Omega Institute. Copyright © 1992 by Robert M. Stein. Used by permission of the author.

"**Sacred Hunger: Shadow, Ecstasy, and Addiction**," is an original essay by Jacquelyn Small, adapted for this volume from the author's book, *Embodying Spirit: Coming Alive with Meaning and Purpose* (San Francisco: Harper/Hazelden, 1994). Copyright © 1993 by Jacquelyn Small. Used by permission of the author.

"**The Moneyed Society**," by Robert J. Sardello, was originally published as "Money and the City," in *Money and the Soul of the World* (Dallas, Texas: Pegasus Foundation, 1983). Copyright © 1983 by Robert J. Sardello. Reprinted by permission of the author.

"**The Scapegoat Archetype**," consists of excerpts (Introduction and Chapter 9) from *The Scapegoat Complex: Toward a Mythology of Shadow and Guilt* by Sylvia Brinton Perera (Toronto: Inner City Books, 1986). Copyright © 1986 by Sylvia Brinton Perera. Reprinted by permission of the author.

"**An Archetypal Dilemma: The LA Riots**," is an original essay written by Jerome S. Bernstein. A shorter version appeared in *Psychological Perspectives* 27 (1992). Copyright © 1993 by Jerome S. Bernstein. Used by permission of the author.

"**Anger Against Children**" and "**Meditations on the Insatiable Soul**" are poems by Robert Bly, © 1994 by Robert Bly. Used by permission of the author.

Nataraj Publishing

is committed to acting as a catalyst for change and transformation in the world by providing books and tapes on the leading edge in the fields of personal and social consciousness growth. "Nataraj" is a Sanskrit word referring to the creative, transformative power of the universe. For more information on our company, please contact us at:

Nataraj Publishing
1561 South Novato Blvd.
Phone: (415) 899-9666
Fax: (415) 899-9667

Other Books and Tapes
from Nataraj Publishing

Books

Living in the Light: A Guide to Personal and Planetary Transformation. By Shakti Gawain with Laurel King. The recognized classic on developing intuition and using it as a guide in living your life. (Trade paperback $9.95)

Living in the Light Workbook. By Shakti Gawain. Following up her bestseller, *Living in the Light.* Shakti has created a workbook to help us apply these principles to our lives in very practical ways. (Trade paperback $12.95)

Return to the Garden: A Journey of Discovery. By Shakti Gawain. Shakti reveals her path to self-discovery and personal power and shows us how to return to our personal garden and live on earth in a natural and balanced way. (Trade paperback $9.95)

Awakening: A Daily Guide to Conscious Living. By Shakti Gawain. A daily meditation guide that focuses on maintaining your spiritual center not just when you are in solitude, but when you are in the world, and especially, in relationships. (Trade paperback $8.95)

Embracing Our Selves: The Voice Dialogue Manual. By Drs. Hal and Sidra Stone. The highly acclaimed, groundbreaking work that explains the psychology of the selves and the Voice Dialogue method. (Trade paperback $12.95)

Embracing Each Other: Relationship as Teacher, Healer and Guide. By Drs. Hal and Sidra Stone. A compassionate guide to understanding and improving our relationships. The follow-up to the Stone's pioneering book on Voice Dialogue. (Trade paperback $11.95)

Maps to Ecstasy: Teachings of an Urban Shaman. By Gabrielle Roth with John Loudon. A modern shaman shows us how to reconnect to the vital energetic core of our being through dance, song, theater, writing, meditation, and ritual. (Trade paperback $9.95)

Notes from My Inner Child: I'm Always Here. By Tanha Luvaas. This deeply touching book puts us in contact with the tremendous energy and creativity of the inner child. (Trade paperback $8.95)

Coming Home: The Return of the True Self. By Martia Nelson. A down-to-earth spiritual primer that explains how we can use the very flaws of our humanness to carry the vibrant energy of our true self and reach the potential that dwells in all of us. (Trade paperback $12.95)

Corporate Renaissance: Business as an Adventure in Human Development. By Rolf Osterberg. This groundbreaking book explodes the myth that a business's greatest asset is capital, and shows why employees must come first for businesses to succeed in the 90s. (Hardcover $18.95)

Passion to Heal: The Ultimate Guide to Your Healing Journey. By Echo Bodine. An invaluable guide to mapping out our individual journeys to health. (Trade paperback $14.95)

The Path of Transformation: How Healing Ourselves Can Change the World. By Shakti Gawain. Shakti gave us *Creative Visualization* in the 70s, *Living in the Light* in the 80s, and now *The Path of Transformation* for the 90s. Shakti's new bestseller delivers an inspiring and provocative message for the path of true transformation. (Trade paperback $9.95)

The Revelation: Our Crisis Is a Birth. By Barbara Marx Hubbard. An underground classic from one of the true prophets of our time. Hubbard offers an astonishing interpretation of the Book of Revelation, which reveals the consciousness required by the human race, not only to survive, but to blossom into full realization of its potentials. (Trade paperback 365 pgs. $16.95)

Tapes

Living in the Light: Read by Shakti Gawain. Shakti reads her best-seller. (Two cassettes $15.95)

Developing Intuition. Shakti Gawain expands on the ideas about intuition she first discussed in *Living in the Light.* (One cassette $10.95)

The Path of Transformation: How Healing Ourselves Can Change the World. Shakti reads her inspiring new bestseller. (Two 70-minute cassettes $15.95)

To Place an Order

Call 1-800-949-1091.